Dedication
To Ruth and Brian Kerry
In appreciation for all
their help

Jonah came from the village of Gath Hepher in Galilee. The Pharisees were wrong therefore when they said to Nicodemus, 'Search and look, for no prophet has arisen out of Galilee' (John 7:52).

But although Jonah was a prophet, the book named after him is not a prophecy, but a biographical narrative involving his prophetic mission to the Gentile Ninevites. I must confess that when I began this book I did not have a very high opinion of Jonah, but all that was to change as the writing process continued. I found him to be a very honest person, believing as I do that he was a historical figure and not a fictional character, prepared to put down in writing his own faults and prejudices so that we might learn from them.

The lessons taught are many, and I hope I have succeeded in drawing out some of them. But the real importance of this little biblical book is its place in God's developing design to embrace both Jew and Gentile in his saving purpose. That design was brought to its grand fulfilment in the gospel of the Lord Jesus Christ. 'But in every nation whoever fears him and works righteousness is accepted by him' (Acts 10:35).

In the process of writing I have come to admire, and even love Jonah in spite of his bigotry and self-will, because of his honesty and truthfulness.

Peter Williams
Bournemouth, 2003

Jonah—running from God

An expositional commentary

Peter Williams

DayOne

© Day One Publications 2003

First printed 2003

ISBN 1 903087 39-2

9 781903 087398

Published by Day One Publications
3 Epsom Business Park, Kiln Lane, Epsom, Surrey KT17 1JF.
01372 728 300 FAX 01372 722 400
email—sales@dayone.co.uk
web site—www.dayone.co.uk
North American—e-mail-sales@dayonebookstore.com
North American web site—www.dayonebookstore.com

Designed by Steve Devane and printed by CPD

Contents

Jonah's character and background

Read Jonah chapter 1:1–2

Who was Jonah, and what kind of man was he? In answer to that it has to be said that we know very little about him, apart from what we are told in the book itself. We know that he lived and prophesied towards the close of the 8th century B.C., and that he came from the village of Gath Hepher in Zebulon of Galilee (2 Kings 14:23–25). Apart from that we have to rely entirely on the narrative itself.

The book does not even claim to have been written by Jonah, but it is my own definite impression, when reading it, that no one but Jonah himself could have been the author. It reads like an honest down-to-earth confession of a man, who—under God's discipline—discovered his own weaknesses and prejudices, and passes on the lessons he has learned from that experience for the benefit of his readers. The narrative even ends with the prophet still lying under the discipline of God's hand as though he is still reflecting, almost in a state of shock, on the distasteful self-truths God has revealed to him. This is meant to teach us to examine ourselves.

Throughout the book the prophet is presented to us as narrow-minded, prejudiced, petulant and aggressively disobedient to God's commands. In view therefore of the high regard with which the Old Testament prophets were held in Israel, as men of God who confronted kings and were active in national affairs, it is highly unlikely that any other Jewish writer would present Jonah in such a bad light. Not that his narrow mindedness and bigotry are the only things to be said about this character. For we find on the one hand that whilst he shows no compassion towards the idolatrous Ninevites, nevertheless on the other hand it is this very zeal for God's honour, and his absolute confidence in God's love and mercy, that prevents him from preaching to them (Jonah 4:2). In that sense it might be said that we can all identify with Jonah as possessing both the weaknesses and virtues that characterise the people of God in every age. But it is his virtues we are meant to emulate, and not his weaknesses.

A real person?

The book has long been a subject of controversy among Bible students, mainly because of its miraculous element, and in particular the miracle of the prophet being swallowed by a great fish. This is a great pity because the fascination with the great fish has meant that many readers have become side-tracked into useless discussions about whether the throat of a whale is big enough to swallow a man, and thereby they lose the essential message of the book. And it does have a *very* positive message containing truths about the relationship between Jews and Gentiles, the missionary task of the church, the compassion of God and his judgement on sin and disobedience, to mention only a few.

Although Jonah was a prophet, the book itself is not a prophecy, but a personal history of God's dealings with his servant. Bible scholars of a liberal persuasion approach the book from the standpoint that Jonah was not even a real person, and they interpret it more as a parable intended to teach certain spiritual lessons. Others have considered it to be a spiritual allegory with Jonah representing the Jewish nation, and his experience of being swallowed by, and delivered from, the great fish as the temporary death and resurrection of the nation under God's discipline.

But the Bible itself leaves us in no doubt whatever that Jonah was a historical person and that he lived during the reign of Jeroboam II towards the close of the 8th century B.C., and prophesied the expansion of the borders of Israel. 'In the fifteenth year of Amaziah the son of Joash, king of Judah, Jeroboam the son of Joash, king of Israel, became king in Samaria, and reigned forty-one years. … He restored the territory of Israel from the entrance of Hamath to the Sea of the Arabah, according to the word of the Lord God of Israel, which he had spoken through his servant Jonah son of Amittai, the prophet who was from Gath Hepher' (2 Kings 14:23 and 25).

Confirmation of the historicity of Jonah also comes from Jesus himself in a reply he gave to the Pharisees who had asked him for a sign. 'An evil and adulterous generation seeks after a sign, and no sign will be given to it except the sign of the prophet Jonah. For as Jonah was three days and three nights in the belly of the great fish, so will the Son of Man be three days and three nights in the heart of the earth' (Matthew 12:39–40). It is inconceivable that Jesus would have used the account of Jonah's deliverance from the huge fish as a sign of such a great historical event as his own resurrection if that account were a fiction. And he goes further in his reply. 'The men of Nineveh will rise up in the judgement with this generation and condemn it, because they repented at the preaching of Jonah; and indeed a greater than Jonah is here' (Matthew 12:41). How could he have said that the Ninevites would rise up at the judgement in condemnation of the people of that generation if they had never existed in the first place? Clearly, our Lord accepted the account of Jonah as historical fact.

One other point needs to be made before we begin our exposition. The book of Jonah holds a unique place in the history of redemption unfolded in Holy Scripture. For whereas other prophets had spoken of God's purpose for the salvation of the Gentile world, Jonah goes a step further and expresses that purpose in action. He actually went to the Gentiles of Nineveh, albeit reluctantly, and preached to them the message of God's judgement which in turn led to their repentance.

The word of the Lord

'Now the word of the Lord came to Jonah the son of Amittai, saying, 'Arise, go to Nineveh, that great city, and cry out against it; for their wickedness has come up before me' (Jonah 1:2).

The expression 'Word of the Lord' is used in connection with the prophets of the Old Testament to indicate both the source of their message and its divine authority. It made clear that it was not their own word or opinion they were giving to the people, but that they were the receivers and communicators of a divine revelation. If Jonah had not received the word directly from the Lord, he himself would never have conceived of preaching to the Ninevites. As it was there was no escaping the fact that this word, with its imperative command, had singled him out personally for a special task. It was as if God had said to him: 'Jonah son of Amittai, I have a special word for your ears only'.

When we read in missionary publications of the lack of Bibles and Christian literature in poor countries, I wonder if we fully appreciate how privileged and blessed we are to receive the Word of God openly and in so many different ways. It comes to us through the regular preaching of the gospel, through Christian books and magazine articles, and through tape and video recordings. Yet with all that, thousands in our own country treat God's word as a matter of total indifference. They willingly listen to the myriad of other voices trumpeting out their message, but turn a deaf ear to what the eternal God has to say about the great issues of life and death.

Such blindness and deafness where God's word is concerned would be incomprehensible were it not that the Bible gives the reasons for it. There is a spiritual deadness in the human heart which, apart from God himself, makes it impossible for a person to even begin to understand the gospel. Paul puts it like this. 'But the natural man does not receive the things of the Spirit of God, for they are foolishness to him; nor can he know them, because they are spiritually discerned' (1 Corinthians 2:14). Or this: 'But even if our gospel is veiled, it is veiled to those who are perishing, whose minds the god of this age has blinded, who do not believe, lest the light of the gospel of the glory of Christ, who is the image of God, should shine on them' (2 Corinthians 4:3–4). The last thing Satan, the god of this world wants, is for people to hear the Word of God and respond to it. Therefore he will do everything in his power to prevent that happening.

In his parable of The Sower, Jesus refers to Satan's strategy in preventing a person from receiving God's word. 'When anyone hears the word of the kingdom, and does not understand it, then the wicked one comes and snatches away what was sown in his heart' (Matthew 13:19). Under Satan's influence people can so easily convince themselves that there is nothing in the message of importance to them, and they will thrust it to one side. It is only God himself, by his Spirit, who can awaken in a person that sense of God-consciousness that enables him or her to listen to the Word of God and take it seriously. That is why we must continue to preach that word in the gospel, for God has promised to honour it. 'For as the rain comes down, and the snow from heaven, and do not return there, but water the earth, and make it bring forth and bud, that it may give seed to the sower and bread to the eater, so shall my word be that goes forth from my mouth; it shall not return to me void, but it shall accomplish what I please, and it shall prosper in the thing for which I sent it' (Isaiah 55:10–11).

The personal word

It is a great blessing when the Word of the Lord comes to us with the personal directness with which it came to Jonah. God singled him out from the crowd with a special word for a special situation. 'Go to Nineveh, that great city, and cry out against it...' And that can happen to us, for God still speaks out of his word to individuals, in a personal manner and directed to their own situation. We can be in a congregation listening to the preaching, or reading the Bible or a Christian book, when suddenly what is said is directed to the heart and conscience and we know without any shadow of doubt that it is the authentic voice of God speaking to us. It may be a word rebuking us for our slackness and lack of zeal in our spiritual life, or a word of comfort and hope if we are going through a difficult experience. It can be so direct and personal that we may feel we are the only one sitting in the congregation.

It sometimes happens that way in the matter of salvation. A person is suddenly convicted of his or her sin as the Word is preached, and in an instant brought to repentance and faith in Christ. The crowd on the day of Pentecost reacted to Peter's preaching in that way. 'Now when they heard this, they were cut to the heart, and said to Peter and the rest of the apostles, "Men and brethren, what shall we do?" Then Peter said to them, "Repent, and let every one of you be baptized in the name of Jesus Christ for the remission of sins; and you shall receive the gift of the Holy Spirit"' (Acts 2:37–38). But, when a person experiences that convicting power of the Holy Spirit, he or she should be careful not to resist and brush it aside as if it were 'all in the mind'. God may not speak in that personal manner to that person again. The Psalmist says: 'Today, if you will hear his voice; do not harden your hearts ...' (Psalm 95:7–8).

Listening to the word

In his letter to the Thessalonian Christians, Paul refers to the way in which different people hear and receive the word of God. 'For this reason we also thank God without ceasing, because when you received the word of God which you heard from us, you welcomed it not as the word of men, but as it is in truth, the word of God, which also effectively works in you who believe' (1 Thessalonians 2:13). There are those who listen to the gospel faithfully preached, and find it interesting, intellectually stimulating, and even helpful and comforting, but it does not authenticate itself to the mind and heart as a divine revelation. That is because they are hearing it only as 'the word of men'.

Now why is that, and how *should* we listen to God's word? In the first place we should remind ourselves that God has already spoken and communicated his word to us through the scriptures, and in his Son the Lord Jesus Christ. 'God, who at various times and in various ways spoke in time past to the fathers by the prophets, has in these last days spoken to us by his Son, whom he has appointed heir of all things, through whom also he made the worlds;' (Hebrews 1:1–2). God's revelation through the writers of the Old Testament reached its finality in the coming of Christ and his gospel. Therefore when we hear the gospel preached on the Lord's day, we ought not to think within ourselves, 'I wonder what this man, this preacher is going to say this morning.' Rather, we should say, 'I wonder what God will reveal to me out of His word this morning?' For Paul says in the passage already quoted, the genuiness of the acceptance of the message as the Word of God is proved by the fact that it is 'at work' in those who believe.

Why Nineveh?

What was the word God gave to Jonah? God said to him, 'Go to Nineveh that great city, and cry out against it; for their wickedness has come up before me.' It reminds us of what God had said centuries before to Abraham concerning the cities of Sodom and Gomorrah. 'And the Lord said, "Because the outcry against Sodom and Gomorrah is great, and because their sin is very grave, I will go down now and see whether they have done altogether according to the outcry against it that has come to me; and if not, I will know"' (Genesis 18:20–21). The result on that occasion was the destruction of both cities as an act of God's judgement.

But why Nineveh? Was it the only city in the ancient world of that time whose people were wicked and godless? No, but it was the most powerful city of its day, and the capital of the mighty Assyrian empire. Its kings and armies were notoriously brutal, even in that barbaric age, and they followed a policy of calculated terror to forestall revolts in the small countries they had subjugated. In 721 B.C. Samaria, the capital of the

Northern Kingdom of Israel, fell to Assyria and was broken as an independent nation, and its people went into exile. In the book of Nahum, which records the fall of Nineveh in 612 B.C., we have a description of her brutality and lust for conquest. 'Woe to the bloody city! It is full of lies and robbery. Its victim never departs. ... Your injury has no healing, your wound is severe, all who hear news of you will clap their hands over you, for upon whom has not your wickedness passed continually?' (Nahum 3:1, 19).

The word of judgement

By Jonah's day Nineveh was sinking in a sea of corruption, and its rulers and people had become so arrogant with pride in their military conquests that God could tolerate it no longer, and commanded his servant to pronounce judgement upon it. This teaches us several things. First, it reminds us that God is the God of history, and that the destiny of men and nations is in his hand. Psalm 2 springs to mind.

'Why do the nations rage,
And the people plot a vain thing?
The kings of the earth set themselves,
And the rulers take counsel together,
Against the Lord and against his Anointed, saying,
"Let us break their bonds in pieces
And cast away the cords from us."
He who sits in the heavens shall laugh;
The Lord shall hold them in derision.
Then He shall speak to them in his wrath,
And distress them in his deep displeasure:
"Yet I have set my King
On my holy hill of Zion."' (Psalm 2:1–6).

Nineveh, like the peoples in that Psalm, represents the anti-God culture and world system which leads men and nations in their pride and arrogance to think they can dethrone God and deify man. But God's law and retribution will not allow men to make a mockery of his justice and moral government of the world. This message runs right through the Bible, beginning with the story of the tower of Babel when the people said: 'Come, let us build ourselves a city, and a tower whose top is in the heavens; let us make a name for ourselves, lest we be scattered abroad over the face of the whole earth' (Genesis 11:4). That intention signifies man's determination to overthrow God's rule and establish his own kingdom and government. But the attempt failed under God's judgement when he scattered the people across the face of the earth.

In the book of Daniel the same truth is emphasised in the account of Nebuchadnezzar's dream in which the statue of gold, silver, bronze and iron—representing the kingdoms of Babylon, Persia, Greece and Rome—is brought crashing down by the stone representing the kingdom of God (Daniel 2:31–45). And although Nineveh repented at the preaching of Jonah, it did not last, and within the next hundred and fifty years it reverted to its former wickedness and pride and was totally destroyed by the Persians in 612 B.C. We learn from all this that nothing man builds in his own strength alone, and in defiance of God's rule and sovereignty in the world, will last for ever. And that includes the political systems of our own day. Hitler's Third Reich, which he claimed would last a thousand years, Lenin's Soviet system which lasted a mere seventy years, and our own British empire, have all come crashing down. So it will be with the world systems, until that day comes when 'the kingdoms of this world have become the kingdoms of our Lord and of his Christ, and he shall reign forever and ever!' (Revelation 11:15).

Presuming on God's patience

The threat of God's judgement upon Nineveh also teaches us that men dare not presume on God's patience regarding sin and wickedness. The secular man may have a vague belief in the existence of God, but to all intents and purposes he lives as a practical atheist, and behaves as if there is no God who is concerned with the moral supervision of the world. But God is not indifferent to what goes on here below, and man's sin does not escape his all-seeing eye. The Bible teaches quite clearly that he will not tolerate man's contempt and rebellion indefinitely, and that he does intervene in history, either in acts of mercy or acts of judgement. These judgmental acts may be described as his interim judgements, leading to his final judgement when history comes to its close.

There are many such interim judgements in the scriptures. Judgement fell on Adam and Eve when they fell into sin and disobedience, and God showed his displeasure by turning them out of the garden. In Noah's time God was so displeased with the wickedness of mankind that he brought judgement in the form of the Flood. In Daniel's time he exercised judgement on King Nebuchadnezzar by removing his reason as a warning against human pride. Belshazzar fell under judgement through the handwriting on the wall. And Jesus foretold the destruction of Jerusalem that occurred in A.D. 70, as God's judgement on the Jewish people. Where Nineveh was concerned, Jonah was to warn its king and people that, because of their lust for conquest and their pride in material strength, God's patience was running out, and unless they came to repentance, judgement was inevitable.

James Philip in his Bible study notes (*Holyrood Abbey Daniel* 1989, page 10) quotes the following lines, which clearly spell out this truth, that man can press God's patience too far.

> 'There is a time, we know not when,
> A place we know not where,
> That marks the destiny of man
> In glory or despair.
>
> There is a line, by us unseen,
> That crosses every path,
> The hidden boundary between
> God's patience and his wrath'.

Nineveh was in danger of crossing that line, and it was Jonah's task, as God's prophet, to draw the people's attention to that fact.

Preaching judgement today

We are living in a day when, because of the godlessness in society, preachers again need to remind people of the judgement of God, both in this life and the next. The gospel must be presented in all its fullness, and it is not enough to speak on the themes of God's forgiveness and fatherly love, and never touch upon the reality of judgement, sin and hell. That is to distort the word of God, and we are explicitly warned in the scriptures against doing that. 'Therefore, since we have this ministry, as we have received mercy, we do not lose heart. But we have renounced the hidden things of shame, not walking in craftiness nor handling the word of God deceitfully, but by manifestation of the truth commending ourselves to every man's conscience in the sight of God.' (2 Corinthians 4:1–2).

We must not be selective in our preaching and use Biblical texts, in Spurgeon's phrase, 'like coat-hangers' on which to hang a few favourite platitudes. It has to be the full word of God in both its saving and judgmental aspects.

Running from God

Read Jonah chapter 1:3–4

When Jonah was commanded by God to go to Nineveh, he did something about it, but it was the wrong thing. He ran away in the opposite direction. 'But Jonah arose to flee to Tarshish from the presence of the Lord. He went down to Joppa, and found a ship going to Tarshish; so he paid the fare, and went down into it, to go with them to Tarshish from the presence of the Lord' (Jonah 1:3). That is a picture of a man running a race he could not hope to win, because it was a race against God. Spiritually speaking, it is a picture of man trying to hide from God's presence, only to find that it is a presence he cannot get away from. Jonah never made it to Tarshish, but even if he had, he would have found that God's presence had beaten him to it.

God's universal presence

One of the important lessons to come out of the book of Jonah is that God is everywhere. This is one of his greatest attributes, and theologians refer to it as the Omnipresence of God. His grandeur and immensity permeate the whole-created order, so that it is impossible to hide from him. Adam tried to do so when he disobeyed God and hid among the trees in the garden. But God found him (Genesis 3:8–10). This truth of God's Omnipresence is one of the great themes of the Bible, and is dealt with in a powerful way by the psalmist.

Where can I go from your Spirit?
Or where can I flee from your presence?
If I ascend into heaven, you are there;
If I make my bed in hell, behold, you are there.
If I take the wings of the morning,
And dwell in the uttermost parts of the sea,
Even there your hand shall lead me,
And your right hand shall hold me.

If I say, 'Surely the darkness shall fall on me,'
Even the night shall be light about me;
Indeed, the darkness shall not hide from you,
But the night shines as the day;
The darkness and the light are both alike to you.

(Psalm 139:7–12).

Men may turn where they will to avoid God's reach and escape his holy presence, but they will always fail. Francis Thompson admirably expresses this truth in his poem *The Hound of Heaven*.

'I fled him down the nights and down the days;
I fled him down the arches of the years:
I fled him down the labyrinthine ways
Of my own mind: and in the midst of tears
I hid from him, and under running laughter.

But with unhurrying chase,
And unperturb'd pace,
Deliberated speed, majestic instancy,
They beat—And a voice beat
More instant than the feet—
'All things betray thee, who betrayest me'.

Thompson is saying that men may try to avoid meeting with God by hiding among the earthly concerns and pleasures of this life, but such things will always let him down and betray him, because he himself has betrayed the Creator of all things. God is the source of all life and being, and therefore there can be no peace, no rest for the soul, until we hide ourselves in him.

Why men hide from God

There are many reasons why people try to hide from God and evade his presence, but let us stay with Jonah for the moment. Why did he flee? Tarshish, after all, was in the opposite direction from Nineveh, possibly off the coast of Spain. He did so because he was not prepared to face up to the demand God was making on him. He was being commanded to do a most difficult and unpleasant thing as a Jew; to preach to Gentiles the hope of repentance towards God. He was perfectly willing to preach to his own people, but it did not fit in with his thinking and prejudice to preach to Gentiles, especially when those Gentiles were the inveterate enemies of his own people. He had no love for Gentiles, and knowing as he did that God was 'gracious and merciful' (Jonah 4:2), and would forgive the Ninevites if they repented, he thought it better to run away and turn his back upon such an unpleasant task.

Is that how we react when God asks us to do the difficult and unpleasant thing? We make our plans and have our lives all neatly arranged, and then God steps in and spoils it all, by asking us to do something that does not fit in with our thinking. How do we respond? Do we 'do a Jonah' and distance ourselves from God by hiding behind a multitude of excuses? Take Moses, he had been living a quiet pastoral life for forty years when God suddenly disturbed his tranquillity by commanding him to set his people free from slavery in Egypt. But he responded in a very negative fashion by making all manner of excuses why he could not do it (Exodus 3–4:17). Or take Jeremiah: when God called him to the prophetic office he responded by saying he could not possibly be a prophet since he was only a youth, and did not have the gift of public speaking (Jeremiah 1:4–8). On the other hand when God commanded Hosea to do what was just about the hardest and most unpleasant thing imaginable, 'Go, take yourself a wife of harlotry and children of harlotry' (Hosea 1:2), he did not try to hide or evade the command, but he actually did it!

And we should all be prepared for God to make hard demands upon us from time to time because that is a part of Christian discipleship. Jesus prepared us for that possibility in his teaching. 'If anyone desires to come after me, let him deny himself, and take up his cross, and follow me' (Matthew 16:24). To the man who wanted to follow him he said, 'Foxes have holes and birds of the air have nests, but the Son of Man has nowhere to lay his head' (Luke 9:58). He was saying, in effect, 'are you willing to give up the legitimate comforts of life to be my disciple?' William MacDonald, who was the Principal of Emmaus Bible School, says this in his booklet on discipleship: 'The Lord Jesus made stringent demands on those who would be His disciples—demands that are all but overlooked in this day of luxury-living. Too often we look upon Christianity as an escape from hell and a guarantee of heaven. Beyond that, we feel that we have the right to enjoy the best that this life has to offer. We know that there are those strong verses on discipleship in the Bible, but we have difficulty reconciling them with our ideas of what Christianity should be.' (*True Discipleship*, Gospel Literature Service, 1963 p. 5.)

The truth is that if we try to hide from God's hard demands we are wasting our time. 'For who has resisted his will?' (Romans 9:19). If he really wants us for some definite purpose he will always get us finally. He is Thompson's *Hound of Heaven*. Jonah, Moses, Jeremiah all gave way in the end, however reluctantly. Far better to make the positive response in the first place like Hosea, or we might have to pay a heavy price for our disobedience. That is what happened to Jonah.

The God who pursues

It seems to me that God sometimes allows us to think that we can hide from him and evade his demands in order to teach us how much we need him, and how much he loves us. For he never gives up on us and will pursue us until we are drawn back to himself. Jonah thought at first that he had made it. Everything seemed to be in his favour when he ran away. He got down to Joppa and there was a ship just about to sail for Tarshish. 'After paying the fare, he went aboard and sailed for Tarshish to flee from the Lord.' As he sailed out of the harbour we can imagine him thinking to himself, 'I have made it! No more wrestling with my conscience about whether I should preach to Gentiles. Peace at last, I can now do my own thing.' But God was in hot pursuit and was not going to let him get away that easily. Jonah was totally unaware of the heavy price he was going to have to pay for running from God's demand—the terrible storm that was to come, the icy water he would be thrown into, and the dreadful experience of being swallowed by the great fish.

The truth was that in spite of his prejudice and disobedience he was still God's man, God's prophet, and once we belong to him he never lets us go, even when we are disobedient and try to evade his demands upon us. He pursues us because he loves us and desires to draw us back to himself. For we are precious to him. Peter puts it like this: 'knowing that you were not redeemed with corruptible things, like silver or gold, from your aimless conduct received by tradition from your fathers, but with the precious blood of Christ, as of a lamb without blemish and without spot' (1 Peter 1:18–19).

This means we cannot lose our salvation when once we have it. When we belong to God in Christ we belong to him for all eternity. This is sometimes referred to as the doctrine of the 'eternal security of the believer'. This is how Jesus put it: 'my sheep hear my voice, and I know them, and they follow me. And I give them eternal life, and they shall never perish; neither shall anyone snatch them out of my hand. My Father, who has given them to me, is greater than all; and no one is able to snatch them out of my Father's hand. I and my Father are one' (John 10:27–30). That is a wonderful promise. If Christ has saved us, then we shall never lose out on heaven and the joy of eternal life. Even when we wilfully disobey his commands, and wander from the path of truth and righteousness, he will not let us go. However hard Satan may try to pluck us out of his hand by urging us to run in the opposite direction, God will always pursue us and draw us back into the way of his love.

God in the storm

'But the Lord sent out a great wind on the sea, and there was a mighty tempest on the sea, so that the ship was about to be broken up' (Jonah 1:4). The wind and the storm were natural phenomena, but the timing of both was in God's hand. He 'sent' the great wind (Jonah 1:4), just as he later 'prepared' a great fish (Jonah 1:17), and 'prepared' a vine (Jonah 4:6), and 'prepared' a worm (Jonah 4:7), and 'prepared' a vehement east wind (Jonah 4:8), all in his pursuit of Jonah. And that is what makes any struggle with God so unequal, he is the God of all creation. 'The sea is his, for he made it; and his hands formed the dry land' (Psalm 95:5). All nature obeys him, for he is omnipotent—all powerful. Run and you cannot out distance him, hide and you cannot be hidden from him, struggle and you cannot overcome him, quarrel and you cannot win the argument. Everything is on God's side.

Clearly this view of creation refutes all other man-made philosophies such as atheism, materialism, humanism and evolution. All these interpretations of life on this planet reject the Biblical teaching of a personal creator, and teach that the universe evolved from properties within itself. No one, least of all God, was responsible for bringing it into being, and therefore we are all at the mercy of mechanical impersonal forces. What a bleak philosophy with which to meet life. And how different from the Bible's message, that behind all the intricate workings of this wonderful world, with its changing seasons and its complex structures of animal and plant life, there is this personal loving God who governs, guides and watches over all things, including his erring children. It is to that God alone that we owe our thanksgiving, our worship and praise.

God's discipline

Poor Jonah, God was really going to put him through it. The storm was only the beginning of his troubles, there was far worse to come—the icy waters and the big fish. For God will not be mocked, not even by his own. There is always a price to pay for running from his demands, for that is how he disciplines and chastens us. Sometimes we can be so wholly absorbed in fulfilling our own objectives, which may be out of God's will, that he will pull us up short through some harsh experience and make us listen to him. That is what he did with Jonah. But in it all God's motive is wholesome and beneficial since he desires only to bring us back into a loving relationship with himself. The writer to the Hebrews puts it like this: 'My son, do not despise the chastening of the Lord, nor be discouraged when you are rebuked by him; for whom the Lord loves he chastens, and scourges every son whom he receives.' (Hebrews 12:5–6).

But we find it hard at times to accept God's discipline, even when it is the result of our disobedience, and we deeply resent it. Jonah was like that. We shall see later that he became very angry and resentful towards God. But it is only when we learn to accept God's discipline that we take the sting out of it. In the above passage the writer to the Hebrews continues: 'Now no chastening seems to be joyful for the present, but painful; nevertheless, afterward it yields the peaceable fruit of righteousness to those who have been trained by it' (Hebrews 12:11).

All this is highly relevant to those who may be passing through a time of spiritual declension or backsliding in their Christian life. For this too is running or hiding from God. For whatever reason a decay of the spiritual life sets in and regular worship, prayer, the reading of God's Word, and fellowship with other Christians become neglected. At first the vacuum left by these things is filled as secular pleasures and interests take over, and all the while the backsliders become spiritually weaker and less able to break the grip of Satan on their lives.

But during this time God is not idle and will not give up on them. After a while this estrangement from him becomes less and less productive. Instead of growing happiness, backsliders become increasingly restless and discontented. They live in a kind of "no man's land", never fully at home in the world since they are still children of God, and never at ease among God's people because they still feel the seductiveness of the world. That is God's doing, for he still pursues them and may even allow them, as he did with Jonah, to go through a very stormy passage in their lives to teach them their need of him. They may even have to get swallowed up, if not by a big fish, then by the sense of hopelessness and despair brought about by circumstances. God may allow them to come to the very end of their resources, so that they are made to throw themselves upon his mercy, and humbly submit to his holy and sovereign will. That was Jonah's experience and we would be wise to learn from it.

Man in crisis

Read Jonah chapter 1:5–6

From what we read in the next few verses it is evident that the storm God had sent in his pursuit of Jonah was particularly violent and the captain and crew of the ship realised they were in great danger with the likelihood of the ship breaking up. 'But the Lord sent out a great wind on the sea, and there was a mighty tempest on the sea, so that the ship was about to be broken up. Then the mariners were afraid; and every man cried out to his god, and threw the cargo that was in the ship into the sea, to lighten the load' (Jonah 1:4–5).

Our modern crisis

What we have in those verses is a picture of men in a time of crisis, and the manner in which they attempt to deal with it. They jettisoned the cargo, but it did not achieve anything, for we read later, 'the sea was growing more tempestuous' (Jonah 1:11), and so their sense of hopelessness was increased. At the spiritual level it is a picture that mirrors the spiritual and moral crisis in our society today, and the futile attempts made to resolve it. Like the ship in the Jonah story the lives of so many threaten 'to break up' because people have rejected God's way of truth and holiness, and have no clear sense of direction and purpose. Without the guidelines laid down in the Bible there are no norms or moral absolutes for people to steer their lives by, and the result is utter confusion. David Wells uses the phrase, 'The weightlessness of God' to describe the 'condition we have assigned him after having nudged him out to the periphery of our secularised life. The engine of modernity rumbles on and he is but a speck in its path' (*God in the Wasteland*, IVP 1994, p. 88).

With the dawn of the new millennium we were confronted time after time on television with displays of man's technological triumphalism, accompanied by promises of a bright new shining world just around the corner. But where is it? What we see in reality is a world lurching from one crisis to another; a world through which the four horsemen of the

Apocalypse are still riding, bringing in their train the devastation of war and violence, of hunger and plague, of death and corruption. Of course, it would be foolish to deny that we have made enormous advances in science, medicine, communications and general standard of living. But at the moral and spiritual level we seem hardly to have advanced at all. With each step forward in the growth of knowledge we create yet bigger ethical problems. We seem trapped in a fiendish web of our own making, and sin continues to do its dreadful work in the world with millions suffering the degradation and brutalities arising out of war and man's inhumanity to man.

Crisis of authority

In many quarters today authority is not a popular word. It is one of those words which is thought to have a distinctly outdated and Victorian flavour about it, and there are those in whom the very symbols of authority, such as the policeman's uniform, stir deep feelings of hatred. Of course we are having to pay a heavy price for this rejection of authority by society, as may be seen in the mindless vandalism in our towns and villages, and in the failure of discipline in our homes and schools.

But apart from this general collapse of authority, it is in the church that it has reached crisis point. The church no longer speaks with the authority of the transcendent Word of God in scripture, and therefore people frequently ignore the message. After all, why should they accept the opinions of the man in the pulpit as carrying any greater weight than those of the politician, the scientist or the philosopher, or for that matter their own ideas and opinions?

The authority of the pulpit that will move and capture the hearts of people is not the preacher's own thinking but the power of the transcendent Word of God in the Bible as the Holy Spirit directs it to the listener. The Bible gives the light of truth concerning the character and nature of God. It tells us that his mercy, love and grace are fully revealed in his Son the Lord Jesus Christ. 'He is the image of the invisible God, the firstborn over all creation' (Colossians 1:15). It also gives the light of truth concerning the nature of the world we live in. We read the newspapers and listen to the news on television to get information about what is happening in the world. But it is the Bible that explains these happenings in the context of the developing history of mankind. And the Bible gives us the light of truth concerning our own human nature. It tells us that man is a fallen being, a sinner deserving only judgement, and that it is his sin that is the cause of all the wrongdoing and unhappiness within himself and his world. But it goes further, and tells us that it is a situation God can remedy through the forgiveness offered in Christ his Son.

If the church were to preach this message more consistently it would recapture the authority it once had, and help to resolve to a large extent the crisis of our time.

The sense of God

'All the sailors were afraid and each cried out to his own god'. The gods these sailors cried out to were only idols, but in the moment of crisis and danger they were forced to reach out beyond themselves to what they believed was a mysterious and superior power that could help them in their distress. This is a primal need in the human heart. Deep within human nature there is this sense of God, or the conviction that there is a superior power or being as the source of life and the controller of all things. Man feels within himself that he is a dependent creature.

Not that he has this feeling all the time, indeed for the most part he hardly thinks about it, and may even deny it altogether, but it lies there dormant within him nevertheless. And as with the pagan sailors in our story, it is when danger threatens, or some crisis looms that he finds himself unable to cope with, that man cries out to the God he believes is there, but does not understand. So why is that? Where does this God-sense come from?

The only sensible answer to that is that God himself put it there in the beginning. We read in scripture: 'So God created man in his own image; in the image of God he created him; male and female he created them' (Genesis 1:27). Unlike the rest of creation man has this spiritual dimension to his being which leads him to ask questions about his own existence and the meaning of what goes on around him in the world. He can think abstractly and logically, and above all, because he is made in God's image, he has an affinity with God and is able to communicate with him in worship and prayer.

Man was made for God, although he may not know it or believe it. And that is the explanation of his restlessness and discontent in this life. He can never be fully satisfied with the things of time, because he is a creature made for eternity. As Saint Augustine says, 'Our hearts are restless until they find their rest in Thee'.

Solving the crisis

When the ferocity of the storm broke, and the ship was in danger of being wrecked, the sailors did the best they could to deal with the crisis—'they threw the cargo into the sea to lighten the load'. But it did not solve anything, since it was only tinkering with the problem, and the crisis remained. 'The sea was growing more tempestuous' (Jonah 1:11).

That is a pretty fair picture of what is happening in relation to the spiritual and moral crisis facing the nation today. Government legislation in crime-prevention acts, more police on the beat, better social programmes, more leisure facilities for our young people, twenty-four hour courts and all the other measures sincerely taken to halt the decline in the quality of life are all worthwhile, but seem to have little effect. It is only tinkering with the problem, which is much deeper because it is to do with fallen human nature.

In a speech at the Guildhall, London, in October 1989, Mrs Thatcher the then Prime Minister said: 'For years when I was young in politics with all the hopes and dreams and ambitions, it seemed to me that if we got an age where we had good housing, good education, a reasonable standard of living, then everything would be set and we should have a fair and much easier future. We know now that that is not so. We are up against the problems of human nature'.

Mrs Thatcher recognised, at least, where the problem lay, although she did not identify it. It is sin in the human heart. And you cannot change people's hearts through legislation alone, or by creating a better environment. Only God's power in Christ can do that. 'Therefore, if anyone is in Christ, he is a new creation; old things have passed away; behold, all things have become new. … God was in Christ reconciling the world to himself, not imputing their trespasses to them' (2 Corinthians 5:17 and 19).

Asleep in the crisis

'But Jonah had gone down into the lowest parts of the ship, had lain down, and was fast asleep' (Jonah 1:5). As Christian believers we feel almost ashamed to read that. In the midst of the crisis the pagan sailors were praying to their gods, who could not help them, and Jonah—the only one aboard who believed in the true and living God—was fast asleep. We can understand that he may have been in need of physical sleep after the stressful time he had been through, but much more serious was the fact that he was asleep spiritually. He was far from God in his spirit of disobedience, and less alert to his presence. The pagans were praying, and God's man was sleeping.

Writing to the Roman Christians Paul urges them to be awake and alert in their spiritual lives in the light of the approaching crisis in the world's history, the Second Coming of Christ. 'Now it is high time to awake out of sleep; for now our salvation is nearer than when we first believed' (Romans 13:11). There is such a thing as spiritual sleep in which the Christian loses his sense of urgency in promoting the gospel and in making progress in holy living. In the garden of Gethsemene when the disciples had fallen asleep the Lord Jesus said to them: 'Watch and pray, lest you enter into temptation' (Mark 14:38). On the mountain of Transfiguration the disciples fell asleep and we read: '…and when they were fully awake, they saw his glory…' (Luke 9:32).

If we want to experience the full glory of the Christian life, then we need to be awake and alert to what God is doing in the world. Lethargy and apathy, like an insidious disease, can creep into the life of the believer deadening his spirit and robbing him of his spiritual energy. The process can begin in small ways, with the neglect of prayer and the reading of God's word, and the falling off in regular worship. And unless we get a firm grip of ourselves and make a real effort of the will, we can easily sink into a state of inertia that is difficult to get out of. And when that happens we are like Jonah, inactive and unproductive, and we are no more than a dead weight to the church and to the cause of God.

Rebuked by the world

'So the captain came to him, and said to him, "What do you mean, sleeper?

Arise, call on your God; perhaps your God will consider us, so that we may not perish"' (Jonah 1:6). This is a sad and shameful picture of a pagan rebuking the man of God, of the worldly man rebuking the Christian. And when it happens it is deeply humiliating, because it ought not to be left to the world to rouse the church to wakefulness in its calling and spiritual responsibilities.

All too often the church loses credibility with the secular man and woman because they see it as no longer taking its own message seriously. People expect the church to give guidance on moral and spiritual matters and to preach the great truths of the gospel, but instead it appears to them that the church's thinking is no different from that in the world around them. In this respect I believe that people have drifted from the church because they feel it has let them down. That is a severe rebuke and should waken us in the evangelical churches to concentrate on getting our priorities right. Let us organise the work and draw up our agendas, but let us not fail to expound God's word and spread the saving gospel of Christ to the lost world.

Some might object that the worldly man is in no position to rebuke the Christian for his moral failings and inconsistencies, since he himself is under the judgement and condemnation of God. But that surely is to miss the point. God can, and does, use every means at his disposal for the correction and discipline of those who belong to him. Writing on this very subject, A.W. Tozer says: 'When reproved, pay no attention to the source. Do not ask whether it is a friend or an enemy that reproves you. An enemy is often of greater value to you than a friend is because he is not influenced by sympathy. Keep your heart open to the correction of the Lord and be ready to receive His chastisement regardless of who holds the whip. The great saints all learned to take a licking gracefully—and that may be one reason why they were great saints.' (Warren Wiersbe, *The Best of A.W. Tozer* Christian Publications Inc 1978, p. 125).

Lastly, we should not get the idea that, because the ship's pagan captain appears in a far better light than Jonah, somehow he was more spiritually minded and therefore closer to God, although he was not aware of it. That is not so. Jonah, for all his faults and disobedience, was God's man and he knew it, whereas the ship's captain was a pagan and had no clear understanding of the eternal God. There are those people who would maintain that the worldly non-Christian who is kind and good-natured and a person of impeccable character and integrity is more Christ-like than many believers. But that is to misunderstand the gospel and to make salvation dependent upon ourselves. But God does not love us and save us because of our integrity and good behaviour, but because we have been cleansed and redeemed by the precious blood of Christ shed on the Cross for our salvation. It is all of grace and nothing of self.

Jonah's profession of faith

Read Jonah chapter 1:7–16

A s the intensity of the storm increased and the sense of crisis deepened, the crew became convinced that their distress was because the gods were angry with someone on board the ship. 'And they said to one another, "Come, let us cast lots, that we may know for whose cause this trouble has come to us"' (Jonah 1:7).

The effects of sin

The sailors were certain that unless they discovered who was the guilty party they would all perish. But the significant thing was that the danger they were in was not because of their own sin directly, but because of the sin and disobedience of Jonah. He was the guilty party, but they, unknowingly, were sharing in the consequences of his guilt. And that is one of the most dreadful aspects of sin, it always involves others apart from ourselves. A person may think, 'It is my life and I can do what I like with it because it only affects me'. But that is not true. We cannot live our lives in complete isolation from others. We are all connected in the bundle of life and we become instruments of good or evil to those around us. My sin causes hurt to others, and we can all, in turn, be affected by the moral atmosphere of the community to which we belong. John Donne the seventeenth century poet expressed it eloquently in a sermon he preached at St Paul's cathedral: *'No man is an island entire of itself; every man is a piece of the continent, a part of the main; any man's death diminishes me, because I am involved in mankind.'*

This thought of our interdependence on each other is especially true of the local church, which is the body of Christ. Paul says 'If one member suffers, all the members suffer with it; or if one member is honoured, all the members rejoice with it' (1 Corinthians 12:26). In the local church, therefore, we will be careful not to adopt an easygoing attitude towards sin and wrongdoing, but will always remind ourselves of the hurt it can do to others in the fellowship. Above all, we hurt God. We 'grieve the Holy Spirit of God' as Paul says in Ephesians 4:30. It will be this consideration, if we keep it in mind, which will overshadow all others and help to keep us from sin and temptation.

Man and destiny

By casting lots the pagan sailors believed that it was possible to know the will of the gods in relation to man's destiny. The actual method involved made use of stones on which names would be written, or coloured pebbles, or sticks of different lengths. But the real significance of what they were doing was the fact that they had a vague belief that there were powers at work in the universe which—in some way or other—determined the destinies of men, and by casting lots they could discover what that destiny was. Now we might be inclined to think that this was just a lot of superstitious nonsense, and yet in an enlightened age like ours there are still millions of people who believe the very same thing.

Take a look at the tabloid newspapers and the glossy magazines, and it will be seen how important it is for many people to know what their horoscope says at the start of the day. Or take the many books and articles on the New Age movement with its emphasis on the Age of Aquarius in the astrological calendar pointing to the ushering in of a transformed world of harmony and 'oneness'. Yet others will turn to other forms of the occult such as spiritism, or mediums and fortune-tellers, to seek some assurance concerning their destiny.

The question is, why do they do it? What is it that drives them to reach out for answers in this way? It is because man has within himself a feeling of restlessness, that things in this world are not as they ought to be, and that he himself is a part of some greater purpose in his own personal life, and in the totality of human existence. He turns to these various things therefore in the hope that they will provide him with a sense of assurance and security by promising an exciting future that will make all his effort and striving worthwhile, and give him the happiness he desires. In short, he wants answers to the mystery of life itself, because he is a creature of destiny. God made him that way.

Christians too want answers, and an inner assurance of their own personal destiny. But unlike the people we have been talking about, believers have no need to be in the dark, or to grope around for answers to these big questions. Like Daniel, in the reply he gave to Nebuchadnezzar who was seeking the meaning of his dream, the believer can say with confidence, 'But there is a God in heaven who reveals secrets' (Daniel 2:28). Through the revelation given in the scriptures, and in the gospel of his Son the Lord Jesus Christ, God has made our human destiny known. For that is what the gospel is in essence—the revealed will and purpose of God for man and his world.

The exposure of guilt

'So they cast lots, and the lot fell on Jonah' (Jonah 1:7). In the light of the context we can hardly believe that it was a coincidence. It is meant to tell us that God is in charge after all, whatever device and method men may use to determine the future. We read in Proverbs 16:33, 'The lot is cast into the lap, but its every decision is from the Lord.

Because he is sovereign there is nothing we can hide from God. When we are out of his will, because we have allowed some sin to break our fellowship with him, then sooner or later he will bring it to light for our own good. He will expose it to our own conscience if we are suppressing it, and—if necessary—he will expose it in the presence of unbelievers. Jonah tried to hide his sin and disobedience, but God exposed it to the pagan sailors through the casting of the lot so as to shame and humble him with a view to repentance. It was all part of God's chastening of his servant in order to draw him back to himself. David tried to hide from God his adultery with Bathsheba, and the murder of her husband Uriah, and he succeeded for a time in suppressing his conscience. But then God exposed his guilt through the parable given by Nathan the prophet (2 Samuel 11, 12). In the case of Peter, God used the cock-crow to expose to his conscience his sin in denying the Lord Jesus (Matthew 26:69–75).

And God will sometimes expose our guilt and weakness to the world because that may be the only way he can awaken our conscience to the seriousness of our predicament, and bring us to repentance and restored fellowship with himself.

Confessing our faith

The moment the lot fell on Jonah exposing his guilt, the sailors began bombarding him with questions. 'Please tell us! For whose cause is this trouble upon us? What is your occupation? And where do you come from? What is your country? And of what people are you?' (Jonah 1:8). Now that he was exposed as the guilty party the crew wanted to know everything about him, his occupation, his race and religion. They were probably under the impression that he had committed some dreadful crime against the gods to bring such a calamity upon them.

In the reply Jonah gives we detect a change of heart, and an element of true repentance towards God. 'So he said to them, "I am a Hebrew; and I fear the Lord, the God of heaven, who made the sea and the dry land."' This terrified them and they asked, 'Why have you done this?' (They knew he was running away from the Lord, because he had already told them) (Jonah 1:9–10). What a relief to find him doing something at last for which we can commend him, instead of being ashamed of him as God's servant. For this was a very bold and open confession of his faith in God, and there are certain things we can learn from it. In the first place he was making his identity known. 'I am a Hebrew; and I fear the Lord, the God of heaven, who made the sea and the dry land.' He did not hide the fact that he was one of God's people, and that says something to us about making our identity known.

Do we hide our Christian faith from others? Is our Christian discipleship something we never like to talk about? If so, why? Does it embarrass us to confess Christ as Lord and Saviour, and are we afraid of the sneers and ridicule of other people? It all comes down to this, in the end. How deep is our faith, and do we love Christ totally? Does he mean more to us than the opinions of other people? Here are four biblical reasons why we should not be afraid to openly publicise our Christian convictions.

(a) Scripture teaches that salvation is only complete and real when it involves both faith and confession. 'That if you confess with your mouth the Lord Jesus and believe in your heart that God has raised him from the dead, you will be saved. For with the heart one believes unto righteousness, and with the mouth confession is made unto salvation' (Romans 10:9–10). We must witness before men that we are one of God's people.

(b) What progress would ever have been made in the work and witness of the church if all Christians through the ages had kept their faith in Christ a secret? It would have been a downright denial of the church's commission given by our Lord himself. 'Go therefore and make disciples of all the nations, baptising them in the name of the Father and of the Son and of the Holy Spirit, teaching them to observe all things that I have commanded you' (Matthew 28:19–20).

(c)   When we are secretive about our Christian discipleship, and fear to own Christ publicly as Saviour and Lord, we hurt and grieve God's Spirit. Paul says, 'And do not grieve the Holy Spirit of God, by whom you were sealed for the day of redemption' (Ephesians 4:30). The Holy Spirit is not an influence but a person capable of being hurt. And we inflict that hurt when we are ashamed of the redemption with which he has sealed us, by keeping our faith a secret.

(d)   Most serious of all Christ tells us that if we are ashamed in a hostile and sinful world to let it be known whose side we are on, then we cannot expect to share in the glories of his kingdom. 'For whoever is ashamed of me and my words in this adulterous and sinful generation, of him the Son of Man also will be ashamed when he comes in the glory of his Father with the holy angels' (Mark 8:38). Far better then to publicly declare Christ as Saviour and Lord now, than to be disowned by him on that final day when he ushers in his kingdom.

The conclusion can only be, that secrecy in discipleship must lead to one of two outcomes. Either the secrecy will kill the discipleship, or the discipleship will kill the secrecy and we shall openly confess Christ as Lord.

Inconsistent faith

In his confession of faith Jonah also makes it clear to the pagan sailors that, unlike their false gods, the God he worshipped is 'the God of heaven, who made the sea and the dry land'. Then the men were exceedingly afraid, and said to him, '"Why have you done this?" For the men knew that he fled from the presence of the Lord, because he had told them' (Jonah 1:9–10). They were terrified because they now understood that behind the storm was the power and greatness of the God of all creation. Their question: 'Why have you done this?' was not an enquiry, therefore, but an expression of amazement and puzzlement that he was so foolish as to disobey—and sin against—such a mighty God! They recognised in their own way the inconsistency between Jonah's profession of faith and his actual conduct.

Does that speak to us as Christians? We believe in Christ in our heart, and we profess him with our mouth, but what about living out our faith in the everyday world? However eloquent a Christian's testimony to his faith in God, it is not likely to impress the worldly person if it is divorced from the practicalities of life. People must see that the gospel works at every level of human activity. It is a shameful evidence of man's sin that in our modern world, where we have the resources and means to ensure that everyone can live decently and with dignity, the problems of poverty, hunger and disease are still with us on a vast scale, and even—in some areas of the world—are getting ever greater. As believers it is an imperative of our faith to help those in need at the personal level, and by our wider support of charitable and Christian causes to feed the poor, to provide medical care, and in general to ease the burdens of our common life. This is love in action as John sees it: 'But whoever has this world's goods, and sees his brother in need, and shuts up his heart from him, how does the love of God abide in him? My little children, let us not love in word or in tongue but in deed and in truth' (1 John 3:17–18).

The mighty creator God

Jonah was right in his confession of faith to stress the majesty of God in creation. 'I am a Hebrew; and I worship the Lord, the God of heaven, who made the sea and the dry land'. This doctrine of God's greatness and power is one that needs to be rediscovered in the present-day church and revitalised in the preaching from our pulpits. All too often God is presented as though he were not that different from ourselves, a kind of super-man figure rather than the might God of the Bible. In a passage of great poetic beauty Job spells out the awesome power of God in creation.

'He stretches out the north over empty space;
He hangs the earth on nothing.
He binds up the waters in his thick clouds,
Yet the clouds are not broken under it.

Chapter 4

He covers the face of his throne,
And spreads his clouds over it.
He drew a circular horizon on the face of the waters,
At the boundary of light and darkness.
The pillars of heaven tremble,
And are astonished at his rebuke.

…

Indeed these are the mere edges of his ways,
And how small a whisper we hear of him!
But the thunder of his power who can understand?' (Job 26:7–11 and 14).

All the miracles and manifestations of God's power that we witness in the realm of creation are, in the end, only the 'edge', a tiny 'glimpse', a mere 'whisper' as it were, of his activity. How then can we ever hope to grasp the fullness or 'thunder' of his great might?

This failure to give the right emphasis to God's majesty and power in our worship and preaching has had serious consequences for the church's witness. Men and women no longer have the fear of God in their hearts, sin has lost its meaning as a radical alienation from God, and there is no longer that sense of accountability before the bar of God's judgement. A further consequence has been that many Christians today have lost heart in the struggle of life. Because their concept of God is so small and meagre their faith has become soft and flabby, unequal to the pressures we are all subject to in today's world. They seem to think that God has lost his grip on things and is as mixed up and confused about life as they are. That is a great pity because it means they are living at a sub-Christian level.

Job was right to say that we can never hope to fully understand God's power. That is something that still awaits us in the future. 'Now I know in part, but then I shall know just as I also am known' (1 Corinthians 13:12). But in the realm of saving grace we have experienced the fullness of divine power in Christ. 'For it pleased the father that in Him all the fullness should dwell, and by him to reconcile all things to himself, by him, whether things on earth or things in heaven, having made peace through the blood of his cross' (Colossians 1:19–20). Unlike Job, how blessed and privileged we are to live on this side of Calvary.

True repentance

The storm continued to rage, and now that they knew Jonah was the cause of it, they consult him as to what they should do next. 'Then they said to him, "What shall we do to you that the sea may be calm for us?"—for the sea was growing more tempestuous. And he said to them, "Pick me up and throw me into the sea; then the sea will become calm for you. For I know that this great tempest is because of me"' (Jonah 1:11–12). Clearly, Jonah had now come to a full acknowledgement of his guilt and disobedience in running from God. And the genuineness of his repentance is seen in his willingness to give up his own life in order to put things right. He could easily have thrown himself overboard, but he wanted it to be a judicial sentence by those he had wronged.

It is possible in the Christian life to use the language of repentance before God, but without having the spirit of repentance in the heart. In short, there is such a thing as spurious or false repentance. The French cynic Voltair once said, 'God pardon? Of course he will, it is His job'. But God will not pardon if the repentance is not genuine.

There are two main characteristics of true repentance. First, there is deep anguish and heartache that one has grieved God's Spirit. Paul describes it as 'Godly sorrow' (2 Corinthians 7:10). It is sorrow for the wrongness of the thing done, not simply regret because of the consequences. In his great penitential psalm expressing his own repentance for his sin with Bathsheba, David says, '… a broken and a contrite heart—These, O God, you will not despise' (Psalm 51:17).

Second, true repentance will always show itself in a change of life and behaviour. We shall see later that Jonah did in fact obey God's command to preach to the Ninevites, albeit reluctantly since he had not yet rid himself of his prejudice towards Gentiles. When John the Baptist appeared along the Jordan he preached a baptism of repentance for the forgiveness of sins. But he was careful to warn the people 'Therefore bear fruits worthy of repentance' (Luke 3:8). And outward confession of sin is never enough in itself, unless accompanied by God-glorifying behaviour.

The impact of faith

Jonah's confession of faith made a powerful impact upon the pagan sailors. Now that they had learned something of Jonah's mighty God, they were reluctant to take the life of his servant by throwing him overboard. 'Nevertheless the men rowed hard to return to land, but they could not, for the sea continued to grow more tempestuous against them. Therefore they cried out to the Lord and said. "We pray, O Lord, please do not let us perish for this man's life, and do not charge us with innocent blood; for you, O Lord, have done as it pleased you." So they picked up Jonah and threw him into the sea, and the sea ceased from its raging. Then the men feared the Lord exceedingly, and offered a sacrifice to the Lord and took vows' (Jonah 1:13–16).

I would not go all the way with those commentators who speak of the sailors' conversion to the God of Israel. But they clearly were deeply affected by Jonah's testimony of faith. We notice that they did not cry out to their own gods as previously, but to the Lord, 'the God of heaven, who made the sea and the dry land', and in thankfulness for being saved from the storm they offered a sacrifice and made vows. What these vows were we cannot say, hence we cannot speak with any certainty of their conversion. But there is no doubt that they were deeply moved by the whole experience and that, in turn, might have led them at a later date to turn to God in faith.

When we give a word of testimony and faith to others, we must believe that God will honour it in some way or other, or there is no purpose in doing it. We might just as well keep our faith secret, as Jonah was inclined to do earlier on. It may not lead to the conversion of those we speak to, but it could make them begin to think seriously about spiritual matters and the needs of the soul. The outcome is entirely in God's hands. The important thing, where we are concerned, is that we do not fail to make our faith known.

The great fish

Read Jonah chapter 1:17

The one thing most people know about the book of Jonah is that it tells the story of a man being swallowed by a whale. But even that is not strictly accurate, for there is no mention of a whale. We are simply told that it was a great fish. 'Now the Lord had prepared a great fish to swallow Jonah. And Jonah was in the belly of the fish three days and three nights' (Jonah 1:17). No indication is given of what species of fish it was, except that the word can be translated 'sea creature' or 'sea monster'. However we cannot leave it at that, because it raises wider questions about the basis of our Christian faith.

The Bible's witness

We said, in the introduction to our opening chapter, that people get so fascinated with the great fish that they miss the real message of the book of Jonah. That is true even of some evangelical Christians, including some preachers. They will go to great pains to try to prove that a whale is capable of swallowing a man, as if the truthfulness of the book's message depended upon it. But that is quite unnecessary, since the book does not mention a whale. But it is also unnecessary for a much more important reason.

The truth of our Christian faith does not depend upon whether we can prove—to the satisfaction of the secular man or woman—the things recorded in the Bible. If that were so we should have to discard the whole supernatural element in the gospel, including the miracles of our Lord, the Virgin birth, the resurrection, the ascension and the Second Coming. We should have to denude the gospel of all these teachings and events since we cannot prove any of them. But then, what would we be left with? Certainly not a gospel, but a mere humanistic philosophy, or—at best a God cut down to our size and convenience. A God who cannot do the impossible and who is no greater than ourselves. But such a God cannot help me in the time of trouble and crisis. He cannot be expected to hear and answer my prayers, or impart the strength that enables me to gain the victory over my circumstances.

No, the validity of our faith and doctrine does not rest on being able to reconcile it with modern day scientific thinking, but on the revelation of God and his Word, and the internal witness of the Holy Spirit. That is something the secular mind cannot be expected to understand. As Paul says, 'But the natural man does not receive the things of the Spirit of God, for they are foolishness to him; nor can he know them, because they are spiritually discerned' (1 Corinthians 2:14). Therefore, when we read that Jonah was swallowed by a great fish we should have no more difficulty accepting that God could accomplish it, than we do in believing that he could raise his Son, the Lord Jesus, from the dead. The internal witness of the Holy Spirit assures us of the truth of both events.

God the preparer

It was no accident that the great fish was in that particular spot in the ocean at the time Jonah was thrown overboard. We are told specifically that 'the Lord had prepared a great fish to swallow Jonah.' This characteristic phrase occurs three more times. In chapter 4: 'And the Lord God prepared a plant' (verse 6); 'But as morning dawned the next day God prepared a worm' (verse 7); 'When the sun arose, God prepared a vehement east wind' (verse 8). Each of these instances was a deliberate act by God to provide for the outworking of his purpose. As the omnipotent God he not only ordains the end, but also provides the means to that end.

This theme of God providing the means for the fulfilment of his purpose runs all through the Bible. He provided the ark for the saving of Noah and his family during the Flood (Genesis 6:14). The title Jehovah-jireh (The Lord will provide) was given by Abraham when God provided or prepared the ram in the thicket to be sacrificed as a substitute for Isaac (Genesis 22:13–14). He provided his people with manna in the wilderness for forty years (Exodus 16:35). When Elijah was hiding in the Kerith Ravine, God provided for the ravens to feed him both morning and evening (1 Kings 17:3–4). In the early days of the church God prepared the way for the spread of the gospel by providing for Philip to meet the Ethiopian on the desert road, who in turn carried the gospel back to his own country (Acts 8:26–40).

In all these instances we are meant to see how God prepares the way, and provides the means for the outworking of his eternal purposes. In the account of Peter's meeting with Cornelius (Acts 10) we have a wonderful example of how God provided for the outreach of the gospel among the Gentiles. At Caesarea the angel appears to Cornelius telling him to send for Peter. Thirty miles away in Joppa, God—through a vision—was preparing Peter's heart and mind in readiness for the meeting. That teaches us that evangelism is not a hit-or-miss affair, but each soul won for eternity is the result of divine planning and preparation, and has its own place in the structure of God's eternal purpose. That should encourage us to see God as the prime mover in evangelism, and not to look upon it as a haphazard business. If he has given us a message for the world, then we must believe—in our preaching and witness—that he has prepared for certain people to receive the message and be brought into his kingdom.

Finally, what of the Cross of Jesus? Was that some kind of afterthought in the mind of God because some other way of salvation had failed? Of course not. It was the final component in the plan of salvation that God had prepared before time began. Christ was 'the Lamb slain from the foundation of the world' (Revelation 13:8).

Jonah as a type

'… And Jonah was in the belly of the fish three days and three nights' (Jonah 1:17). God has made known his revealed will to us in the Bible, not only through its clear doctrinal teaching, but also in the use of figures of speech including symbols, metaphors, emblems and types. A type is meant to foreshadow or point forward, by way of illustration, to some greater truth or reality in God's Word. But we have to be very careful that we do not press the type too far. Some Christian writers are guilty of going to exaggerated lengths in their attempts to see anticipations of the person and work of Christ in their exposition of some of the Old Testament narratives, and in so doing they undermine the credibility of typology.

But in the case of Jonah inside the great fish we are on safe ground, because the Lord Jesus himself used it as a type of his own death, burial and resurrection. The Pharisees had asked for a miraculous sign and he replied: 'An evil and adulterous generation seeks after a sign, and no sign will be given to it except the sign of the prophet Jonah. For as Jonah was three days and three nights in the belly of a great fish, so will the Son of Man be three days and three nights in the heart of the earth' (Matthew 12:39–40). Jesus is here making Jonah the type, and himself the great antitype.

But one other point needs to be made before we go any further. Like all types and analogies, that between Jonah's deliverance from the great fish and Christ's deliverance from the grave is not perfect, since it breaks down in one important respect. Christ refers to his dead body in the grave, and that raises the question whether Jonah actually died when swallowed by the great fish. Some writers are quite emphatic that he did. 'By implication then, if Jonah was miraculously kept alive at "the bottom of the mountains" for "three days and three nights", he was a true sign of Jesus in his death, burial and resurrection. This is why we hold that Jonah actually died and that God brought up his life again from corruption' (Herbert Lockyer, *All the Messianic Prophecies of the Bible,* Pickering & Inglis 1974 p. 259).

I find Lockyer's conclusion hard to accept since, in chapter two, Jonah recalls in great detail the prayer he offered, whilst in the great fish and no one else we know of in scripture recalls their experience in death.

Death and resurrection

When Jesus referred to Jonah's experience in the great fish he described it as a 'sign'. A sign— any sign—is intended to tell us something, to impart information. So what do we learn from Jonah's experience as a sign of the death and resurrection of the Lord Jesus Christ?

First, when Jonah was swallowed by the great fish one would naturally assume that that was the end for him. Nothing would seem to be more final. And yet, after three days and three nights, he was alive and well having been delivered by the mighty power of God (Jonah 2:10). In the same way, when men saw the Lord Jesus being swallowed up in the earth at his burial, they thought that was the end. But it was not the end where God was concerned. His mighty power was at work, and after three days Jesus rose again. As Paul puts it, he was 'declared to be the Son of God with power according to the Spirit of holiness, by the resurrection from the dead' (Romans 1:4). Just as Jonah was delivered from his watery grave to continue the work of preaching repentance and salvation to the Ninevites, so Christ through his resurrection continued—through the gift of the Holy Spirit to the church—to preach the gospel of salvation to the whole world.

For the last word is never with men, but with God. Throughout history men have tried to destroy and bury the work and witness of the gospel; and at times they have succeeded, and have congratulated themselves that that was the end. But God's power was at work and it has always come to life again. Witness what happened in the old Soviet Union under communism when the church was persecuted, believers imprisoned, and the Bible outlawed. God's power was at work and it came to life again. The same happened in China when Christian missionaries were expelled and the church closed down. Many then thought that that was the end of the great vision of Hudson Taylor, but God was at work, and today there are more believers in China than ever before. The last word is never with men, but with God's power.

Second, Jonah's 'burial' for three days and three nights in the great fish was God's judgement on his sinful disobedience. For God hates sin, and his holiness demands that he deals with it. After Jonah had undergone that judgement, God delivered (resurrected) him from the great fish because his justice was now satisfied. Jonah's experience, therefore, was a true type of Christ's own death on the Cross, followed by his burial and resurrection for our justification. His death was a propitiation of God's wrath and judgement on sin, and the satisfaction of his justice. But the analogy between Jonah and Christ is not perfect, since Jonah suffered for his own sin, whereas Christ suffered on the Cross for our sins.

Look at it this way. Job at one point asks the question: 'But how can a man be righteous before God?' (Job 9:2). To be righteous before God means to be right with God, to be reconciled and at peace with God, to know that—although you are not sinless—nevertheless God accounts you as if you were. But how do we obtain that state of 'rightness' in our present sinful condition? For we have already said that God's nature is such that he hates and abhors evil. Habakkuk says of God: 'You are of purer eyes than to behold evil, and cannot look on wickedness' (Habakkuk 1:13).

The Good News of the gospel is that God himself has provided in Christ's death on the Cross a propitiation for our sins, so that we might be justified in his sight. Paul puts it like this: 'For he (God) made him who knew no sin to be sin for us, that we might become the righteousness of God in him' (2 Corinthians 5:21). At Calvary the wrath and judgement of God that should have come upon us, because of our sins, fell upon God's Son so that we could be cleansed and forgiven.

Third, God's purpose in providing for Jonah to be swallowed by the great fish, and then to be ejected, was that he might fulfil the original commission to preach repentance and salvation to the Gentile Ninevites. The barrier of his personal prejudices and Jewish narrowness towards Gentiles was broken down by God's power. In that respect he is once more a type of the Lord Jesus. It was through Christ's death on the Cross, and his resurrection, that the barriers separating Jew and Gentile through the ages were broken down. Prior to Christ's coming the Jew had nothing but contempt for Gentiles, but all that was to change with the coming of the gospel. Paul—the great apostle to the Gentiles—states it in this way. 'Therefore remember that you, once Gentiles in the flesh—who are called Uncircumcision by what is called the Circumcision made in the flesh by hands—that at that time you were without Christ, being aliens from the commonwealth of Israel and strangers from the covenants of promise, having no hope and without God in the world. But now in Christ Jesus you who once were far off have been brought near by the blood of Christ. For he himself is our peace, who has made both one, and has broken down the middle wall of separation, having abolished in his flesh the enmity, that is, the law of commandments contained in ordinances, ... (Ephesians 2:11–15).

Jonah the type and Christ the antitype were both the means, through God's power, of opening the door for Gentiles into the kingdom of God.

Inside the great fish

Read Jonah chapter 2:1–3

There is a limit to the things you can do when you are trapped inside a great fish. So Jonah did the one thing that is more important than anything else a person can do, whether inside a great fish or anywhere else—he prayed 'to the Lord his God from the fish's belly' (Jonah 2:1). When you think of it that is the wonderful and unique thing about prayer, you can do it any time, in any place, alone or in company, verbally or in silence.

We said earlier that some writers (Herbert Lockyer, *All the Messianic Prophecies of the Bible,* Pickering and Inglis, 1974, p. 259) maintain that Jonah died physically when he was swallowed by the great fish, and was brought back to life when the fish disgorged him. But we suggested then that that would mean he would have had to recall his experience of praying when he was actually dead, and that seems highly unlikely. In all probability the thoughts underlying the prayer were in his mind and heart during his time in the great fish, but the actual words and imagery of the prayer were written after his deliverance. This would also help to explain why certain phrases and images in the prayer are strongly reminiscent of the kind of language found in some of the psalms. As a prophet and devout Jew, Jonah would have been familiar with the psalms.

For example the Psalmist frequently speaks of the deep, the waters, the floods, billows and waves to express great distress and despair. '… all your waves and billows have gone over me' (Psalm 42:7). Or this: 'The pangs of death surrounded me; and the floods of ungodliness made me afraid. The sorrows of Sheol surrounded me; the snares of death confronted me. In my distress I called upon the Lord, and cried to my God; he heard my voice from his temple, and my cry came before him, even to his ears' (Psalm 18:4–6).

Why pray?
Of the four chapters in the book of Jonah, chapter two is devoted wholly to

the prophet's prayer. That in itself must say something to us about the importance and urgency of prayer. In the book of Job chapter 21:15 the wicked man says: 'Who is the Almighty, that we should serve him? And what profit do we have if we pray to him?' Many would go along with that. Prayer is a useless exercise. But that is not the view of the Bible which sees prayer as the highest activity of the human spirit.

Why pray? First, because we are commanded to in God's word. In the passage on prayer in the Sermon on the Mount Jesus introduces it with the words: 'And when you pray'. (Matthew 6: 5). He takes it for granted that his followers pray and that prayer is a regular part of their daily lives. In the parable of The Persistent Widow (Luke 18:1–8), the reason Jesus gives for telling it to his disciples is, 'that men always ought to pray and not lose heart'. The words 'always ought' carry with them the force of a command. Paul urges his readers to 'pray without ceasing' (1 Thessalonians 5:17), and James says 'Draw near to God and he will draw near to you' (James 4:8). That coming near can be at any time and in any place. For Jonah it was from inside the great fish.

Second, we pray as Christians because it is necessary and needful. We may not understand everything about the mechanics of prayer, since there is an element of mystery about it, and it raises some perplexing questions, but nevertheless we feel the inward urge to do it. We feel the need and even the urgency at times, to 'come near' to God as James says. That is because our soul and spirit cannot do without it, any more than our body can go without food.

And it is not only the Christian who may feel that necessity. During the second world war there was a common saying in the armed forces: 'there are no atheists in foxholes', meaning that when in combat a man is hiding in a hole in the ground with shells bursting all around him, he would suddenly find himself praying, although he may never have prayed in his life before. And almost any pastor will say that in visiting a hospital he has had someone reach out a hand and say: 'please say a prayer for me'. Why do people do it when normally it would be the last thing to enter their minds? Is it because they find in prayer a psychological release in the time of crisis by expressing their emotions of fear or thankfulness? I do not know, but they feel the urge to do it. What we can say is, that for the believer, prayer is much more than a psychological necessity or a form of emotional release, it is a spiritual need. After all, the non-Christian does not know who he is praying to, whereas the believer is not simply uttering words to someone he hopes might be 'up there', but he is talking to his heavenly father in a meaningful and direct way.

A third reason for praying is because we are actually strengthening God's hand, as it were, in the warfare against the forces of evil and darkness in the world. Speaking of this Paul says: 'For the weapons of our warfare are not carnal but mighty in God for pulling down strongholds.' (2 Corinthians 10:4). The strongholds he has in mind are those of Satan in the world, and the prayers of believers are one of the mighty weapons in the arsenal of God for their destruction. William Cowper expresses the same thought:

> 'Satan trembles when he sees,
> The weakest saint upon his knees'.

Compelled to pray

Up to this point Jonah had been anything but prayerful in his life. Why had he not prayed earlier when aboard ship? The pagan captain was angry with him because he was more concerned with sleeping than praying. 'So the captain came to him, and said to him, "What do you mean, sleeper? Arise, call on your God; perhaps your God will consider us, so that we may not perish"' (Jonah 1:6). The truth was Jonah—through his disobedience—was out of step with God and had therefore neglected the discipline of prayer. But now things had changed. He was in a desperate personal situation inside the great fish, and he was driven to pray. 'He said: "I cried out to the Lord because of my affliction, and he answered me. Out of the belly of Sheol I cried, and you heard my voice"' (Jonah 2:2).

Let us make no mistake about it, prayer, wonderful and great a privilege though it is, is nevertheless a discipline we have to impose upon ourselves if we want it to enhance our spiritual life. It is not something we should engage in spasmodically or when we 'feel' like it. Our prayer life needs to be regular, structured and disciplined. When Darius the king issued a decree forbidding anyone to pray to their god for a period of thirty days we read: 'Now when Daniel knew that the writing was signed, he went home. And in his upper room, with his windows open toward Jerusalem, he knelt down on his knees three times that day, and prayed and gave thanks before his God, as was his custom since early days'(Daniel 6:10). That tells us that Daniel had a regular, disciplined prayer life, and it was that, I believe, that helped him to withstand the loneliness and pressure of high office in a pagan country, and to retain his faith in the true God.

If we pray only when we feel like it then our spiritual life will suffer. For let us be perfectly honest, we all have times when we simply do not feel like praying. Almost any pastor has had a member of his church tell him that their Christian life seems to be all dried up and uninspiring and that they no longer enjoy reading the Bible or having a regular prayer time. The reason is simple. Like Jonah they have neglected the discipline of prayer, and are like a man trying to live on a minimum of oxygen, they are lifeless, inwardly dried up and spiritually apathetic because prayer is the oxygen of the soul and we need it in regular doses.

The other thing here is this. Jonah only got back into the discipline of prayer because God compelled him to through his situation. Look at his words: 'I cried out to the Lord because of my affliction ... Out of the belly of Sheol I cried' (Jonah 2:2). He was in a bad way and God was the only one he could turn to. And that can happen to us. We may go for days or weeks or months without praying and then something happens, some personal crisis, which fills us with a sense of helplessness, and we are driven to our knees to call out to God. Our praying then is not so much a matter of choice as a compulsion God uses to show us our need of a disciplined prayer life. But why wait for that to happen? Far better to undertake the discipline now and be able to face the crisis when it comes.

Prayer heard and answered

Jonah's prayer was both heard by God and answered. 'I cried out to the Lord because of my affliction, and he answered me' (Jonah 2:2). The answer is given in the last verse of the chapter. 'So the Lord spoke to the fish, and it vomited Jonah onto dry land'. That is one essential fact concerning prayer that we ought never to lose sight of, that God always hears the prayers of his people and listens to their cry. Jonah says: 'Out of the belly of Sheol I cried, and you heard my voice.' Isaiah says: 'before they call, I will answer; and while they are still speaking, I will hear' (Isaiah 65:24). When Daniel was praying for understanding of the vision the angel said to him: 'Do not fear, Daniel, for from the first day that you set your heart to understand, and to humble yourself before your God, your words were heard; and I have come because of your words' (Daniel 10:12).

So we must never think that God has not heard our prayer, or that he is aloof and disinterested when we speak to him. That is never the case. God is a loving heavenly Father and like a father he listens to what we have to say to him. In the book of Revelation we have a wonderful picture of this truth. 'When he opened the seventh seal, there was silence in heaven for about half an hour. … Then another angel, having a golden censer, came and stood at the altar. He was given much incense, that he should offer it with the prayers of all the saints upon the golden altar which was before the throne. And the smoke of the incense, with the prayers of the saints, ascended before God from the angel's hand' (Revelation 8:1–4). Here is the silence of reverence in heaven that God may hear and receive the prayers of his people.

Perplexities about prayer

In the light of what has been said two objections might be raised. First, some Christians are perplexed as to the purpose of prayer. They recall that Jesus said: 'And when you pray, do not use vain repetitions as the heathen do. For they think that they will be heard for their many words. Therefore do not be like them. For your Father knows the things you have need of before you ask him' (Matthew 6:7–8). If God knows what we need where is the point of praying? Well, Jesus is saying that we have no need to pray for everything in our lives. We do not normally begin each day by asking God to supply our food, clothing, shelter, health and the countless other things that are a part of daily life. We thank him for these things, but we have no need to ask for them for he knows how necessary they are to our well-being.

But in his wisdom there are some things God has decided to give us only in answer to prayer. It may be the need for guidance, or special faith in some circumstance, or strength to overcome a particular temptation. Having to ask for these things reinforces our dependence upon God and serves to emphasise the important place prayer should have in our lives. As James puts it: 'Yet you do not have because you do not ask' (James 4:2).

Second, Christians have no difficulty in believing that God hears our prayers, and also that he answers prayer, as he did with Jonah. But what about the prayers that are not answered? I am not sure we can unravel this one completely, but there are some things to be said which may help us to live with this difficulty and be at peace. First, we have to accept the fact that God, in his father-like wisdom, sometimes says No, and we simply have to accept the negative response as his answer. Sometimes we may ask for something that is not in line with his will, for John says 'if we ask anything according to his will, he hears us' (1 John 5:14). Or we may pray from a wrong motive says James: 'You ask and do not receive, because you ask amiss, that you may spend it on your pleasures' (James 4:3). Then again the answer seems to be No when in fact God is simply delaying the answer for some reason known only to him. An example of that is the story of Zacharias and Elizabeth in Luke's Gospel. They had prayed earlier in their lives for a child, but nothing happened. Then, when they were old an angel appeared to Zacharias and said: 'Do not be afraid, Zacharias, for your prayer is heard; and your wife Elizabeth will bear you a son, and you shall call his name John' (Luke 1:13). Commenting on this verse Matthew Henry, the old Puritan commentator, says: *'Prayers of faith are filed in heaven and are not forgotten, though the thing prayed for is not presently given'*. So the thing to keep in mind in all this is, unless we receive a definite negative from God we should keep on praying and wait patiently for God's own time.

Honesty in prayer

Jonah was very honest and humble in his prayer and recognised that his present position was the result of his own disobedience and sin, and that God had judged him because of it. 'For you cast me into the deep, into the heart of the seas, and the floods surrounded me; all your billows and your waves passed over me' (Jonah 2:3). We know from chapter one that it was actually the crew of the ship who had thrown Jonah overboard at his own request. But here he acknowledges that behind it all was the hand of a sovereign God who was punishing him because of his sin and disobedience. That is why he uses expressions like, '*You* cast me into the deep,' and 'Into the heart of the seas, and the floods surrounded me; All *your* billows and *your* waves passed over me' (Jonah 2:3).

There is a spirit of true repentance and humility in the prayer that makes it acceptable to God. In recalling his prayer from inside the great fish Jonah is telling us that he rightly deserved what was happening to him, but that God had shown him great mercy. This explains why the prayer contains no request to be delivered from the danger he was in, but is wholly a prayer of thanksgiving and praise because God did in fact deliver him—verse 9 makes that clear: 'But I will sacrifice to you with the voice of thanksgiving'. So what do we learn from all this?

Well, it tells us that there is a right way to approach God in our prayers. We have to be honest and open with him, holding nothing back. If there is anything in our life to be confessed, then we should confess it otherwise God will not hear us. The Psalmist is emphatic on this. 'I cried to him with my mouth, and he was extolled with my tongue. If I regard iniquity in my heart, the Lord will not hear. But certainly God has heard me; he has attended to the voice of my prayer' (Psalm 66:17–19). Then again we must be very humble in the way we approach God. Earlier, Jonah had been terribly arrogant in his attitude towards God and thought that he could outwit him by turning his back upon him and going off in the opposite direction, thinking he could out distance God. But he learned to his great cost that you can not play games with God like that. God must be God. In his prayer Jonah humbly recognises that fact by acknowledging the sovereign character of God in what had happened to him.

There is a balance to be struck in this matter of our approach to God. The scriptures teach us on the one hand to be bold and confident in our praying: 'Therefore, brethren, having boldness to enter the holiest by the blood of Jesus, by a new and living way which he consecrated for us, through the veil, that is, his flesh, …' (Hebrews 10:19–20). But at the same time we must never forget that it is the Eternal Sovereign God we are speaking to. Intimacy with God in prayer must never degenerate into familiarity. He is the Creator, we are the creatures. He is in heaven, we are on earth. In the words of Abraham (Genesis 18:25, 27) He is 'the judge of all the earth', we are 'but dust and ashes'.

Cast out by God

Read Jonah chapter 2:4–7

W e said earlier that certain phrases in Jonah's prayer are strongly reminiscent of the language in the Psalms. This is particularly true of the section we are now considering, but there is nothing strange in that since we should expect a devout Israelite and prophet, like Jonah, to be familiar with the metaphors and word pictures with which the Psalms abound. His entombment in the great fish must have been a terrifying ordeal, especially since he must have been conscious the whole time, or else he would not have been able to remember his prayer. Looking back on the experience later he says it was like being in the subterranean world of the dead. 'Out of the belly of Sheol I cried, and you heard my voice' (Jonah 2:2). The Psalmist uses a similar picture: 'The sorrows of Sheol surrounded me' (Psalm 18:5).

A hopeless situation

In our present passage Jonah continues with deep intensity to describe the horrors of his situation. 'The waters surrounded me, even to my soul; the deep closed around me; weeds were wrapped around my head. I went down to the moorings of the mountains; the earth with its bars closed behind me forever' (Jonah 2:5–6). Jonah does not use this poetic language for its own sake, but transfers the thought forms of the psalms to his own literal situation inside the great fish. Speaking of the Psalms, Calvin says: 'Not without good grounds am I wont to call this book an anatomy of all parts of the soul, since no one can experience emotions whose portrait he could not behold reflected in its mirror'. This is certainly true of Jonah's phrase, 'the earth with its bars closed behind me forever' which perfectly describes his emotion of total hopelessness and despair. The word 'bars' refers to the bars of the city gate in ancient times. Jonah felt that the gate or doorway back to the earth was securely locked and barred against him forever. Never again would he return to life on the earth.

We can surely understand Jonah's sense of utter hopelessness, since although we have never had the experience of being inside a great fish, many will have had such a severe hammering from life at times that it has crushed any vestige of hope we may have had. Like Jonah we felt that the door to God's presence was barred against us, and there was no way out of our circumstances. When that happens it can create a real problem for the Christian. We may feel on the one hand that we should be able to say, 'Things are in a bad way, but I still have my faith in a loving God, and I "know that all things work together for good to those who love God, to those who are the called according to his purpose"' (Romans 8:28). But it is not easy to say that when life has hammered you into the ground. And then the problem is compounded because we feel ashamed and guilty that, as a child of God, we cannot say it.

I have written about this elsewhere and can do no better than repeat what I said then. 'The question is, ought we as Christian believers to feel ashamed of such feelings? I do not think so, because it is a part of our God-given humanity. We are not machines or robots, but we have emotions and feelings capable of being hurt by the harsh realities of life. We need to remember that, because there are some Christians who feel guilty when they become depressed and downcast and think in themselves, "I should not be feeling like this, I am a child of God and this is wrong". But such thinking only aggravates the condition of hopelessness. The truth is that different factors can contribute to our state of mind, such as sickness or personal temperament. The important thing is to handle it in the right way' (*Insights into Job*, Day One, 2002, p. 27).

But what *is* the right way to handle this kind of spiritual depression? To begin with we should not dwell on our condition and allow Satan to exploit it to the point where it becomes an obsession with us, and we lapse into a state of morbidity. We must look away from ourselves and to God. After all, hopeless as Jonah's situation seemed to be, God did in fact rescue him. 'Yet you have brought up my life from the pit, O Lord, my God' (Jonah 2:6). And the Psalmist, when he experienced similar feelings of depression, cried out: 'Why are you cast down, O my soul? And why are you disquieted within me?' But as if he suddenly remembered God's presence he followed it quickly with: 'Hope in God; For I shall yet praise him, the help of my countenance and my God' (Psalm 42:11).

The Bible is quite clear that there are no hopeless situations with God, there are only hopeless people in those situations. And we must hold on to that, for that is the essential difference between the Christian and the non-Christian in the face of life's struggles. The non-Christian may have the superficial optimism which enables him to believe that somehow everything will turn out all right in the end. But that is all he does have, and it rests on the very shaky foundation of his own power and resources alone. But the believer has the God of all power and comfort on his side. That same power which brought out of the darkness and seeming hopelessness of Calvary, the light and hope of the resurrection, is our power and our hope.

Forsaken by God

Jonah's emotions inside the great fish were in turmoil. Not only did he feel a deep sense of hopelessness engulfing him, but also even more terrifying was the awful thought that God himself had forsaken and abandoned him. 'I said, I have been cast out of your sight; …' (Jonah 2:4). How long that feeling lasted we cannot say, because it did pass eventually, his hope revived, and he was able to say, 'yet I will look again towards your holy temple' (Jonah 2:4), meaning that he had an inner assurance that he would worship again in God's house. But as long as his feeling of abandonment by God lasted, whether long or short, it must have been a dreadful experience for him, as God's servant, to see himself as banished, and cast out beyond God's sight.

He was well aware, of course, that it was his own sin and disobedience that had brought about his separation from God. Earlier, when he had taken a ship to Tarshish, he was fleeing from God, but now God had fled from him. For that is what sin does, it brings us under the discipline of God's judgement, and makes us feel that God no longer loves us, and does not care about us. We become alienated from him. This feeling was not peculiar to Jonah's experience. David, in his penitential Psalm, involving both the guilt of his adultery with Bathsheba and his murder of Uriah, expresses his greatest of all fears, that he would lose the presence of God's Spirit. 'Do not cast me from your presence, and do not take your Holy Spirit from me' (Psalm 51:11).

Now the question has to be asked: Does God ever forsake, or cast out from his sight, those who truly belong to him? There is a sense in which it does happen, but not on a permanent basis. Also, when it does happen, it is not related to the loss of our salvation, but to the loss of our fellowship with God. As David puts it in the above Psalm: 'Restore to me the joy of your salvation, and uphold me by your generous Spirit' (Psalm 51:12). It was not his salvation he had lost, but the joy and fellowship with God that goes with it. This sense of alienation, or abandonment, is one of the ways in which God disciplines us because of our sin and disobedience, and teaches us not to take his presence for granted. Or else God may allow it to happen to us in order to test and strengthen our faith in him.

It is an experience as old as man himself, and in the Bible we find men of great faith asking, in effect, the frightening and bewildering question: 'Where has God gone?' The Psalmist cried out on one occasion: 'Why do you stand afar off, O Lord? Why do you hide in times of trouble?' (Psalm 10:1). And what about Job? It was one of his bitterest complaints in the midst of all his trials, that God had deserted him. 'Even today my complaint is bitter; my hand is listless because of my groaning. Oh, that I knew where I might find him, that I might come to his seat! I would present my case before him, and fill my mouth with arguments...Look, I go forward, but he is not there, and backward, but I cannot perceive him; when he works on the left hand, I cannot behold him; when he turns to the right hand, I cannot see him' (Job 23:2–4 and 8–9). It was all such an agonising experience for poor Job.

But the one encouraging thing in all this is that, in spite of our real feelings in the dark moments of life that God has abandoned us, in actual fact he never does. Spurgeon once saw a weathercock with the text: 'God is love', and said to his companion that he did not think it was very appropriate on such a changeable thing as a weathercock. But his companion said that he had misunderstood its real meaning which was, that 'God is love' whichever way the wind blows (quoted by Griffith Thomas, *Epistle to the Romans,* Eerdmans Publishing, 1946, p. 232). And that is true. Whichever way the wind blows in our lives, for good or ill, God is there watching over us, and if our fellowship with him is broken because of our sin and disobedience, then repentance will always bring forgiveness and the restoration of his presence. Jonah recognised that, since hard on the heels of his sense of abandonment came the positive conviction: 'yet I will look again towards your holy temple'. For a devout Israelite like Jonah the temple was the meeting-place with God, and he was convinced that once again he would enter the sanctuary.

And let us not forget in all this, such positive statements in scripture as: 'For he himself has said, "I will never leave you nor forsake you"' (Hebrews 13:5), or Paul's magnificent statement in Romans about God's love to us in Christ. 'For I am persuaded that neither death nor life, nor angels nor principalities nor powers, nor things present nor things to come, nor height nor depth, nor any other created thing, shall be able to separate us from the love of God which is in Christ Jesus our Lord' (Romans 8:38–39).

Man's rejection of God

But there is another more serious aspect to all this. So far, we have been talking about the Christian believer. But what about the non-Christian? Is he or she abandoned by God in the sense that they can reach a position where they have no hope of salvation or forgiveness? The Bible's answer is an unequivocal 'yes', as long as that person remains in a state of unbelief and rejection of God. That surely is the profound and frightening truth taught in Romans: that when men deliberately forsake God through the perversity of their own minds, they subject themselves to being forsaken by God and incurring his wrath and judgement. Three times Paul, in chapter one, uses the expression, 'God gave them over' when referring to the depravity of man's thinking and behaviour.

'Therefore God also gave them up to uncleanness, in the lusts of their hearts, to dishonour their bodies among themselves' (Romans 1:24). 'For this reason God gave them up to vile passions. For even their women exchanged the natural use for what is against nature' (Romans 1:26). 'And even as they did not like to retain God in their knowledge, God gave them over to a debased mind, to do those things which are not fitting' (Romans 1:28). It is as if God said to men: 'so you think you can govern and control your lives without me? Very well, I will take off the restraints of sin and we will see what will happen'. And we all know only too well the mess that men have made of life in this world without the controlling hand of God.

In the Old Testament we have the same truth taught in connection with the story of the Flood. 'Then the Lord said, "My Spirit will not strive with man forever…"' (Genesis 6:3). God was announcing beforehand that the period of his saving grace, before Judgement would come on mankind, was running out. For in the same chapter we read: 'Then the Lord saw that the wickedness of man was great in the earth, and that every intent of the thoughts of his heart was only evil continually. And the Lord was sorry that he had made man on the earth, and he was grieved in his heart. So the Lord said, "I will destroy man whom I have created from the face of the earth…"' (Genesis 6:5–7), Human depravity had so increased that God withdrew his Spirit, not because he was unwilling to save mankind, but because mankind refused to be saved.

The warning to people today is clear. This is still the day of God's grace, and the door to salvation through Christ is still open. But a day will surely come when the door will be shut; the day of God's grace will have passed, and for those who refused to enter there will only remain the prospect of God's condemnation. Little wonder the writer to the Hebrews reminds us: 'It is a fearful thing to fall into the hands of the living God' (Hebrews 10:31).

Remembering God

In verse 7 we come to a significant turning point in Jonah's experience inside the great fish—he remembered God. 'When my soul fainted within me, I remembered the Lord; and my prayer went up to you, into your holy temple'. Earlier he had forgotten God, and had even deliberately kept God out of his thoughts by trying to get away from him. But his present predicament had changed all that, for he now remembers God, and the memory stirred in him a need to pray, and to direct his thoughts heavenwards to God's temple or dwelling place.

The faculty of memory is strange and mysterious, and can be either a curse or a blessing. We all have memories that bring joy to our hearts, and those that make us sad. We have memories that can lift up our spirits, and others that drive us into a pit of depression. We have memories that can inspire us, and those that torment us. Jonah remembered God, and it inspired him to pray with profound thankfulness. Peter on the other hand remembered, and the memory tormented him. 'The Lord turned and looked at Peter. Then Peter remembered the word of the Lord, how he had said to him, "Before the rooster crows, you will deny me three times". So Peter went out and wept bitterly' (Luke 22:61–62).

There is in all of us that tension between the things we want to forget but keep on remembering, and those things we want to remember but keep on forgetting. And it is our failure, even as Christians, to straighten out this tension that hinders our spiritual lives. It seems to me that Joseph, in the Old Testament story, got it just about right. 'And to Joseph were born two sons before the years of famine came, whom Asenath, daughter of Poti-Pherah priest of On, bore to him. Joseph called the name of the firstborn Manasseh: "For God has made me forget all my toil and all my father's house." And the name of the second he called Ephraim: "for God has caused me to be fruitful in the land of my affliction"' (Genesis 41:50–52).

'God has made me forget all my toil'. He did not mean that the memory of past happenings was erased from his mind, but that God helped him to forget the bitterness and hurts associated with the past events of his brother's hatred, his near-death experience in the pit, his enslavement and his unjust imprisonment. And when such bitter memories insist on pushing themselves to the surface of our minds, God can help us through prayer to take the sting out of them. Similarly Joseph says, 'God has caused me to be fruitful in the land of my affliction'. He remembered his present blessings of his elevation in Egypt and the joy of home and family life. And we have equal cause to remember God's goodness in the blessings of daily life.

This thought concerning the memory of God's goodness is one the Psalmist brings home to us very forcefully. 'Bless the Lord, O my soul, and forget not all his benefits' (Psalm 103:2). But the sin of forgetfulness is exactly what we are so often guilty of. We can become so absorbed in the rush of daily life and with our personal concerns that we forget to praise God for his benefits, perhaps for days or even weeks on end. Not that we deliberately forget or put the thought of God out of our minds; but neither do we make any real effort of the will to remember. And if we should wonder what those benefits of God are that we should make the effort not to forget, the Psalmist mentions some of the more important ones in the following verses.

'... who forgives *all* your iniquities' (Psalm 103:3). Not just some of them but all of them! He reaffirms it in verse 10: 'He has not dealt with us according to our sins, nor punished us according to our iniquities'. If God did treat us as our sins deserve we would not last five minutes in his sight. But in Christ he forgives all our sins. 'For he (God) made him who knew no sin to be sin for us, that we might become the righteousness of God in Him' (2 Corinthians 5:21).

'... who heals all your diseases' (Psalm 103:3). That does not mean we shall never be ill again. God can, and does, heal the body, but we must remember this is the praise of the soul. When God forgives and saves us that is not the end of the matter but the beginning. It takes the rest of our lives for the Holy Spirit to sort out and sanctify the diseases and disorders in our personalities. There is a lot of inner healing to be done from self-centredness, envy, pride, lack of stability and love of worldliness. But God can do it, and through the Holy Spirit he seeks to bring us daily more into the likeness of Christ.

'... who redeems your life from destruction, who crowns you with lovingkindness and tender mercies' (Psalm 103:4). Jonah thankfully remembered that God had brought him out of the pit of despair and hopelessness. 'Yet you brought up my life from the pit, O Lord, my God' (Jonah 2:6). Many Christians will have cause to remember how God, in his grace, brought them out of the pit of loneliness or depression. But all believers have cause to remember that God delivered them from the pit of sin and destruction and set their feet on the rock Christ Jesus.

> In loving-kindness Jesus came,
> my soul in mercy to reclaim,
> and from the depths of sin and shame
> through grace he lifted me.

'... who satisfies your desire with good things so that your youth is renewed like the eagle's' (Psalm 103:5). It pays us to remember that God not only saves and keeps us, but he fully satisfies. He brings fullness into our lives. It was believed in the ancient world that the eagle renewed its strength and vitality in the moulting season. That work of spiritual renewal is taking place in us. Paul says, 'Even though our outward man is perishing, yet the inward man is being renewed day by day' (2 Corinthians 4:16). As the body steadily moves downwards to death and the grave, so the soul moves steadily upwards to the eternal presence of God. What wonderful benefits these are, and how we should make a real effort of the will not to forget them, but to keep them always in the forefront of our thinking.

True and false religion

Read Jonah chapter 2:8–10

In these closing verses of Jonah's prayer we come to its climax in which he makes a great confessional statement of his absolute faith in the one true God. 'Those who regard worthless idols forsake their own mercy. But I will sacrifice to you with the voice of thanksgiving; I will pay what I have vowed. Salvation is of the Lord.' (Jonah 2:8–9).

There are three things in that statement which had deeply impressed the mind and heart of Jonah during his experience inside the great fish, and from which we can all learn something. There is the peril and worthlessness of idolatry, the importance of keeping the vows we make, and the solid conviction that salvation is to be found in God alone.

Idolatry

'Those who regard worthless idols forsake their own mercy'. Why this reference to idolatry? Some commentators suggest that Jonah had in mind the pagan sailors he had met earlier on board the ship, and whose prayers had been offered to their false gods. But that is doubtful, if only because he had every reason to be very grateful to them. After all, they had treated him with great kindness, and had done their level best to save his life by rowing back to land. No, the real reason why idolatry surfaced in his thinking was, I believe, because in the great fish he had come close to death, and to the fresh realisation of God's faithfulness and goodness, as opposed to the sheer emptiness and futility of everything else in this life in which men put their faith and hope. Earlier, when he was running from God he had, for a while, forgotten that great truth, but now he asserts it with renewed conviction in his heart. He had reflected on the fact that men 'forsake their own mercy' from God, when they look to anything other than to the one true God for the hope of salvation. He makes a positive statement to that effect: 'Salvation is of the Lord.'

Lying vanities

In the Authorised Version the phrase used of idolaters in this verse is 'they that observe lying vanities'. That is an almost perfect description of what idolatry really is. False religion is a vain lie. It holds out the promise of good, but always it fails to deliver. It is worthless and deceptive, a delusive fantasy. In Jonah's day such false religion took the form of worship given to graven images of wood or stone, or molten images such as the golden calf (Exodus 32), and the devotion associated with sacred pillars and sacred trees.

God's prophets in the Old Testament, like Isaiah, poured scorn on these objects of veneration, and spoke of them contemptuously as nonentities or 'nothing'. 'Who would form a god or mold an image that profits him nothing? ... He burns half of it in the fire; with this half he eats meat; he roasts a roast, and is satisfied. He even warms himself and says, "Ah! I am warm, I have seen the fire." And the rest of it he makes into a god, his carved image; he falls down before it and worships it, prays to it and says, "Deliver me, for you are my god"... And no one considers in his heart, nor is there knowledge nor understanding to say, "I have burned half of it in the fire, yes, I have also baked bread on its coals; I have roasted meat and eaten it; and shall I make the rest of it an abomination? Shall I fall down before a block of wood?"' (Isaiah 44: 10, 16–17, 19).

But whilst the prophets treated these false gods with such contempt, they nevertheless recognised that, behind these physical representations of deity, there were powerful demonic forces at work, which is what makes idolatry both wrong and dangerous. In the New Testament, Paul says exactly the same thing by way of a warning against idolatry. 'What am I saying then? That an idol is anything, or what is offered to idols is anything? Rather, that the things which Gentiles sacrifice they sacrifice to demons and not to God, and I do not want you to have fellowship with demons' (1 Corinthians 10:19–20). We must not entertain the idea therefore that, because we no longer worship wood or stone idols or sacred trees and pillars, we—in our civilised sophisticated society—are not idolaters. The fact of the matter is that there is as much, even more, idolatry and worship of false gods in our society today as ever there was in the time of Jonah. The demonic powers behind false religion are still very much at work in people's lives, blinding them to the worship of the one true God.

Modern Idolatry

For we must ask again, what is the essence of idolatry? It is anything that commands the central place in our lives, and to which we give the loyalty and devotion, which rightly belongs to God alone. This means that the principle of idolatry can include just about everything. In his letter to the Colossians Paul gives a list of things, all of which he denounces as idolatry. 'Therefore put to death your members which are on the earth: fornication, uncleanness, passion, evil desire, and covetousness, which is idolatry' (Colossians 3:5). For some people money is their god, and the pursuit of materialistic goals dominates their lives. In this country alone we spend forty billion pounds annually on gambling, and the government is presently considering further liberalisation of our gambling laws. But we can make an idol of anything, sport, sex, drugs, politics, career, even home and family. Anything that nudges God out to the perimeter of our lives can become idolatrous.

Millions today worship at the shrines of false gods, but they all share the main feature of false religion in every age—they are the product of man's own mind and imagination. For that very reason they can be of no spiritual use to him because they are an extension of his own weakness and failings. As Jonah says, they become worthless 'lying vanities', and will always let man down, because—however much he tries to manipulate them for his own happiness—they will always fail to deliver in the long run what they promise.

There is one other important aspect to all this. John ends his letter with the affectionate warning to his readers: 'Little children, keep yourselves from idols' (1 John 5:21). Those early Christians were surrounded by physical idols of all kinds in the pagan temples, but John's real concern was about the pagan influences some of them were bringing into the Christian fellowship. And a lot of that is happening today. Evangelical Christians are being influenced by the secular spirit and thinking of our age. This is a form of idolatry, and a mixing of the truth with the false. Worldliness is the curse of a number of churches today. And, if we look further, we find that in our multi-faith society church leaders are perfectly willing to widen out the ecumenical debate by including other religions in which idols, icons and other physical representations of deity are venerated and worshipped.

Evangelical Christians must strongly resist going down that path, because the Bible expressly forbids it. 'I am the Lord your God...You shall have no other gods before me. You shall not make for yourself a carved image—any likeness of anything that is in heaven above, or that is in the earth beneath, or that is in the water under the earth; you shall not bow down to them nor serve them...' (Exodus 20: 2–5). That is a very definite statement of the exclusiveness of the worship of God alone. And the New Testament is equally positive. 'For there is one God and one mediator between God and men, the man Christ Jesus' (1 Timothy 2:5).

Keeping your vows

'But I will sacrifice to you with the voice of thanksgiving; I will pay what I have vowed.' (Jonah 2:9). How faithful are we in making good the vows and promises we make to God? When we are in trouble, or find ourselves hemmed in by a really difficult situation, it is the easiest thing in the world to vow that, if God will hear our prayer and get us out of our predicament, we will serve him more faithfully in the future. But do we keep that vow when the crisis passes and life is all milk and roses again?

Making the vow is the easy part, keeping it is far more difficult, as is evident from the thousands of broken marriage vows every year with all the unhappiness and guilt that can ensue. Jonah's thanksgiving and sacrifice were associated with the vow he had made when inside the great fish. Now that he had been delivered he was determined to keep that vow. 'I will pay what I have vowed'. What was that vow? Whilst we are not told in so many words, we may take it that it was a vow of deeper commitment to God's service. After all, he had lost that sense of commitment to his prophetic calling when he had refused to go to Nineveh. Later, as we shall see, he was still reluctant to obey the command, but he nevertheless did so and therefore kept his vow.

In the Bible we have several instances of people making vows and it is instructive to see the different attitudes they adopted.

Jacob's vow

One of the earliest examples is Jacob's vow following his dream at Bethel. 'Then Jacob made a vow, saying, "If God will be with me, and keep me in this way that I am going, and give me bread to eat and clothing to put on, so that I come back to my father's house in peace, then the Lord shall be my God. And this stone which I have set as a pillar shall be God's house, and of all that you give me I will surely give a tenth to you'" (Genesis 28:20–22).

Commentators differ in their interpretation of this vow, and some see it as Jacob's wily brain seeking to strike a bargain with God. But that does not fit in with the rest of the story. Following his dream Jacob had a profound sense of holy fear and he would hardly have adopted such a shabby and irreverent attitude towards God. Furthermore God had already promised him in the dream, 'I am with you and will watch over you wherever you go' (Genesis 28:15). In using the word 'if' Jacob was not doubting God's word but was saying in effect: 'since God has promised to be with me and bless me then I in turn promise that he will always be my God'. It was in short a vow of commitment and, although God had to discipline him many times before he finally fulfilled his vow, there came a point where God changed his name from Jacob (deceiver) to Israel (overcomer) (Genesis 32:28).

Samson's vow

Samson's attitude to the Nazarite vow, taken at his birth, was totally different. He was careless and indifferent. It was meant to be a vow of separation (Numbers 6:1–8), but he failed dismally to live up to it. He was separated to God outwardly, but not inwardly, and even when the Spirit of God came upon him, enabling him to perform great feats of strength, his essential wilful character remained unchanged. Samson paid a heavy price for breaking his vow, and he is a warning to believers that our commitment to Christ is meant to set us apart spiritually from the lifestyle and values of the secular society in which God has set us.

Jephthah's vow

Jephthah's vow (Judges 11:30–35) was absurd and foolish, and he ought never to have made it. He promised God that, if he gave him victory over the Ammonites, he would sacrifice in thanksgiving whatever came first out of the house to greet him on his return. He certainly was not thinking of his only child, a daughter, but that is what happened. She was the first to greet him and he felt bound to keep his vow. It was a vow that brought tragedy, and was rashly and thoughtlessly made. He had no need to bribe God with such a promise for the purpose of defeating the enemy, since God had already promised him the victory.

Hannah's vow

Hannah, on the other hand, made a sacrificial vow and kept to it (1 Samuel 1). She had longed to have a child, especially a son, and vowed that if God would answer her prayer she would dedicate him to the Lord's service. When Samuel was born she did just that. It was a great sacrifice to give back to God what she loved most, and wanted to keep in her life, but she did it.

Making a vow before God such as is implied in ordination, marriage, baptism, church membership, or in committing one's life to Christ is a very serious matter. It should not be done thoughtlessly and without counting the possible cost involved, for God will one day hold us responsible. Jesus had something to say about this, which we should take on board. 'You have heard that it was said to those of old, "You shall not swear falsely, but shall perform your oaths to the Lord." But I say to you, "Do not swear at all". .... But let your 'Yes' be 'Yes' and your 'No' 'No'. For whatever is more than these is from the evil one"' (Matthew 5:33–37).

We may wonder what is the relevance of what Jesus is saying here to the question of vows and promises? Well, we must understand in the first place the purpose of an oath. When the name of God was used in an oath it was meant to buttress, or give added solemnity to, the truthfulness of the vow or promise that was made. And that is perfectly in order provided we really mean what we are saying, otherwise we are taking the name of God in vain. 'If a man makes a vow to the Lord, or swears an oath to bind himself by some agreement, he shall not break his word' (Numbers 30:2). Jesus therefore is emphasising the need for truthfulness in what we say, whether it is in the form of a vow or promise, or in anything else we say. But the Scribes and Pharisees to whom he was speaking maintained that if the name of God was not used in the oath, then it was not all that serious if the vow or promise was broken, or a lie spoken. It was this flippant disregard for truth that Jesus was condemning when he said, 'Do not swear at all'. In other words, it is better not to make a vow or promise if we do not intend keeping it, or we may incur God's wrath.

This has something to say to us as Christian believers. We are not to engage in the double talk and the lies and deceit that characterises so much of the talk and conversation of the world, even by those in authority who make public pronouncements. It is against that evil that Christ exhorts us to say what we mean, and to mean what we say, with simple truthful 'yes' or 'no'.

Salvation

After all God had put him through Jonah was led to express his deepest and most profound conviction in the simple confession: 'Salvation is of the Lord'. But what exactly did he mean by his use of the term 'salvation'? Clearly he must have had in mind the actual physical deliverance from inside the great fish, mentioned in the last verse of this chapter. 'So the Lord spoke to the fish, and it vomited Jonah onto dry land' (Jonah 2:10). Incidentally, this seems to be the only pleasant use of the word 'vomit' in the Bible. But then it really was a pleasant and wonderful deliverance from the great fish of which Jonah could say, 'salvation is of the Lord'.

But the prophet's use of the term went much deeper than that. Salvation is a basic theme of the whole Bible, and in the Old Testament it was extended and deepened to include the saving activity of God in many different situations. It is used of the national salvation of Israel from bondage in Egypt (Exodus 14:30); of the deliverance from disease (Isaiah 38:20), and of the deliverance God affords to the poor and needy (Psalm 34:6). Jonah's use of the term included not only physical deliverance, but salvation from every kind of spiritual evil. He had already voiced his conviction that 'Those who regard worthless idols forsake their own mercy' (Jonah 2:8), meaning that when men put their trust and hope in anything other than the eternal God, they cut themselves off from the one and only source of spiritual life and salvation in the forgiveness of their sins.

Christ's salvation

When we turn to the New Testament, it is the spiritual aspect of salvation and deliverance that predominates, and is centred in the death and resurrection of the Lord Jesus Christ. Doctrinally speaking it is perfectly acceptable for the Christian to speak of salvation in three tenses. He can say, 'I have been saved', 'I am being saved', and 'I shall be saved'.

For the Christian to say, 'I have been saved', is to recognise God's saving action in history in the person of Jesus Christ who is 'the lamb slain from the foundation of the world' (Revelation 13:8). That means that, even before man fell into sin in the Garden of Eden, God had already laid down the plan of salvation that would restore man to a state of grace through the atoning death of Christ on the Cross of Calvary. Preaching on the day of Pentecost Peter refers to God as the source and origin of our salvation in Christ when he says: 'Him, being delivered by the determined purpose and foreknowledge of God, you have taken by lawless hands, have crucified, and put to death' (Acts 2:23). It is clear from Peter's words that we are not to interpret our Lord's death on the Cross as simply the outcome of powerful religious and political forces in first century Jerusalem, or as the martyrdom of a good and holy man. On the contrary, it was the sacrifice for sin which God, in his foreknowledge, had purposed before the beginning of time. And that is what makes our personal salvation the awe-inspiring experience it really is; that God the Eternal planned it even before the dawn of creation. As Paul says: 'Just as he chose us in him before the foundation of the world, that we should be holy and without blame before him in love' (Ephesians 1:4).

For the Christian to say, 'I am being saved' means that he has not only been saved from the guilt of past sin, but that he is being saved from the pollution and the power of sin in his life at the present time. We read in 1 Corinthians, 'For the message of the cross is foolishness to those who are perishing, but to us who are *being* saved it is the power of God' (1 Corinthians 1:18). Here and now we share in the risen glorified life of Christ who by his Spirit sanctifies us, and enables us by His power to live a life of holiness. In one of his hymns Charles Wesley puts it perfectly in the line: 'He breaks the power of cancelled sin'. Covered as we are by the righteousness of Christ our sin is cancelled, wiped out in God's sight. But as long as we remain in this sinful world sin still wields a power in our lives, but with the help of the Holy Spirit even that tyranny can be broken, and as Wesley says in the next line: 'He sets the prisoner free'.

For the Christian to say, 'I shall be saved' means that our salvation will only be complete when Christ comes again, and on that resurrection morning our very bodies as well as our souls will be redeemed from sin. In this sense it is still futuristic and is the thought underlying those words of Paul: '... now our salvation is nearer than when we first believed' (Romans 13:11). At the resurrection our bodies will be changed and we shall be completely delivered from sin in every respect. 'Now this I say, brethren, that flesh and blood cannot inherit the kingdom of God; nor does corruption inherit incorruption. Behold, I tell you a mystery: we shall not all sleep, but we shall all be changed—in a moment, in the twinkling of an eye, at the last trumpet. For the trumpet will sound, and the dead will be raised incorruptible, and we shall be changed. For this corruptible must put on incorruption, and this mortal must put on immortality' (1 Corinthians 15:50–53). That will be our final glorification, to be like Christ.

Jonah said, 'Salvation comes from the Lord'. Of course it does, since only God could accomplish all that!

Jonah's second chance

Read Jonah chapter 3:1–4

In these verses we come to a new chapter in the personal history of Jonah. Up to this point we have seen him as a man rebelling against God, running from God, being pursued by God, praying to God, and finally being delivered by God. In all these experiences he had learned many lessons, and had received new insight into a number of truths concerning his own character and the character of God.

But now that we are in a new phase in the prophet's life, we have every reason to believe that he is a humbled and chastened man, and profoundly thankful that, by God's grace, he is restored and forgiven. But that is not the end of the matter. There is still the question of his prophetic calling. Is that now over? Has he, by his wilful rebellion and sinful disobedience, barred himself from ever again being God's mouthpiece and a servant of his Word? For up till now he had hardly measured up to the ideal of a prophet of the Lord.

Renewed opportunity for service

For my own part it is with a sense of relief that I read: 'Now the word of the Lord came to Jonah the second time, saying, "Arise, go to Nineveh, that great city, and preach to it the message that I tell you"' (Jonah 3:1–2). Not only was he restored and forgiven, but God reinstated him to the prophetic office. Many of us would surely admit that we see something of ourselves in Jonah when we reflect upon our failures in service and Christian discipleship. How many of us, each in his or her own way, have pursued our own shabby little schemes outside of God's will, and been wilful enough to sacrifice all too often the noblest virtues of faith, truth, and integrity on the altar of personal expediency? And when that has happened, and we have lost our testimony in the eyes of others, we have had the nagging feeling that we were all 'washed-up' in the ministry and service of the Lord. Is our sphere of usefulness over? Will God ever trust us with the responsibility of his work again? We are restored and forgiven, yes, but what of our work for God?

We have no idea how long a period lasted between Jonah's deliverance from the great fish, and the Lord's coming to him a second time. It may have been days, weeks, months or even years. In the meanwhile it was a time of waiting, and Jonah may even have gone back to his home village of Gath Hepher feeling that his usefulness in God's service was over. He may have thought to himself, 'How can God use me now, after the shabby way I have treated him? I have been a rotten prophet and a disgrace to my office'. And then he might have settled down to see what would be the next move. This is mere speculation of course, but underlying it is the truth that when one has had the privilege of serving God in a special capacity, waiting to get back into action can be especially difficult. But if, for whatever reason, we have to wait upon God we need to be careful that we do not get frustrated, and give way to the temptation to hurry things up a bit by taking some short cut to attain our goal. God has his own time-scale, and we must be willing for him to initiate the next move.

The problem today

Now all this raises a very important question concerning ministry and Christian service today. We are living at a time when the low moral standards of secular society have steadily crept into the Church, and into the lives of ministers of the gospel, church leaders and church workers. I can remember being at a minister's conference some years ago and sharing in a heated discussion on this very subject. The discussion centred on whether it would be right and wise for anyone guilty of a serious lapse of moral standards to take up the work of the ministry again.

I recall that some present were adamant in their conviction that such a privilege should be forfeited. Others, myself included, were less certain and felt that it should be left to the individual and God, but that there should be true repentance and a period of waiting for God's leading. And I am convinced that this is the right approach in the light of Jonah's experience. And there are other examples in scripture. Abraham acted wilfully and sinfully when he could not wait for the promised son Isaac, but married Hagar who gave birth to Ishmael and laid the foundation for the deep hatred and dissension between Jew and Arab in middle east politics today. But God forgave him, and continued to use him mightily in his service.

David let God down badly by his adultery with Bathsheba and the murder of Uriah, but God forgave him and continued to make him a key figure in the history of Israel. Peter, likewise, let the Saviour down when he denied him three times, but the Lord forgave him and made him the leader of the apostolic band.

In the light of the above the advice to anyone caught in a similar situation must be, repent fully before God, and wait patiently for him to take the initiative in coming 'a second time' to provide the opportunity for renewed service.

God's unchanging purpose

When theologians speak of God's Immutability, they simply mean that he does not change. This is an aspect of God's character that meets us all through the Bible, and is of more than academic and theological interest. To know that God is always the same imparts confidence to our faith, and assures us that he is to be utterly relied upon even in the most critical situation. But not only is God unchanging in himself, his word is unchanging, his promises are unchanging, and his purpose is unchanging.

When God came to Jonah the second time, the instruction he gave him was the same as the first time. 'Arise go to Nineveh, that great city, and preach to it the message I tell you'. God had not changed his mind about the Ninevites, and his purpose for them was the same; they were to hear his word. We see from this that behind Jonah's disastrous failure, God was in perfect control of events. For when he has a purpose to fulfil, nothing is allowed to frustrate that purpose in the long term—not Jonah's failure, not our failures, not the machinations of men, nor the forces of evil at work in the world. Satan may have his own evil designs to thwart God's purpose, and he may even succeed in the short term, for he does have his 'little season' (AV) or 'little while' to wreak havoc in the world (Revelation 20:3). But ultimately there is nothing that can prevent God's purpose from coming to fruition in the unity of all things in the Lord Jesus Christ.

God does not work at random, or in fits and starts, moving in one direction only to change his plan or purpose in the next generation. Speaking through his servant Isaiah God says: 'Remember this, and show yourselves men; recall to mind, O you transgressors ... For I am God, and there is no other; I am God, and there is none like me. Declaring the end from the beginning, and from ancient times things that are not yet done, saying, My counsel shall stand, and I will do all my pleasure' (Isaiah 46:8–10). And we read in Ephesians: 'having made known to us the mystery of his will, according to his good pleasure which he purposed in himself, that in the dispensation of the fullness of the times he might gather together in one all things in Christ, both which are in heaven and which are on earth—in him. In Him also we have obtained an inheritance, being predestined according to the purpose of Him who works all things according to the counsel of His will' (Ephesians 1:9–11).

We learn from the Old Testament that in the beginning God had a purpose for mankind in the creation of Adam, but through his disobedience sin entered the world, and wickedness grew to such an extent that God brought the human race to an end through the Flood (Genesis 7). But God's purpose did not change, he simply carried on that saving purpose through Abraham to whom he said 'And in you all the families of the earth shall be blessed' (Genesis 12:3). Next he brought the Jewish people into a covenant relationship with himself to be his agency in the world. But the Jewish nation failed to carry that purpose through. But it made no difference; God simply carried on his purpose through bringing the Church into being at Pentecost. In the gospel of his Son he is still calling a people for his own to be his agency in the world, until that day when his purpose will be fulfilled with the termination of human history at the coming again of Christ to this world, when he will usher in the 'new heavens and a new earth, in which righteousness dwells' (2 Peter 3:13). What a scenario! And how glorious to think that we believers are a part of that great saving purpose of God.

To come back to Jonah, God had a saving purpose for the people of Nineveh, and although Jonah messed it up by his disobedience, it made no difference. God's purpose was the same and he would see it through.

The message given

When God came to Jonah the 'second time', he gave him the clear instruction that he was only to proclaim to Nineveh 'the message that I tell you'. That was wise advice, not only for Jonah, but also for all preachers. As

God's servant and spokesman Jonah was not to exercise his own powers and discretion as to what he would say to the people of Nineveh. God had given him the message, and that was the message he was to preach, and nothing else.

So it is with today's preacher. There is a very real sense in which his message has already been given him by God. He does not have to invent his message, nor is he in the pulpit to give out his own ideas for changing people's lives, and to make a better world. It is the preacher's task and privilege to declare, as clearly and as powerfully as God will enable him, the truth revealed in the Bible and in the person of Jesus Christ—the word made flesh. Indeed, during his earthly ministry, Jesus emphasised again and again that he could only declare the message given him by his Father. 'For I have not spoken on my own authority; but the Father who sent me gave me a command, what I should say and what I should speak. And I know that his command is everlasting life. Therefore, whatever I speak, just as the Father has told me, so I speak' (John 12:49–50).

Dr Jim Packer defines preaching as follows. 'Its content is God's message to man, presented as such. For the evangelical, this means that the source of what is said will be the Bible, and furthermore that a text will be taken (a verse, a part of a verse, or a group of verses), and the truth or truths presented will be, as the Westminster Directory for Public Worship put it, "contained in or grounded on that text, that the hearers may discern how God teacheth it from thence." The preacher will take care to make clear that what he offers is not his own ideas, but God's message from God's book, and will see it as his task not to talk for his text, but to let the text talk through him' (J.I. Packer, in the introduction to 'Preaching', Presbyterian and Reformed Publishing Company, 1986, p8).

Good, solid, biblical preaching or exposition is the great need of today, and it will involve a good deal of hard work on the part of the preacher in studying, essential reading and—above all—prayer. We are living at a time when the preacher feels pressurised by the changes taking place in society, and is tempted to shape his message to fit in with those changes. But the word of God does not change, and that is what gives authority and power to the message, and enables men and women to know true freedom and forgiveness to be able to cope with life in the modern world.

Urban evangelisation

'So Jonah arose and went to Nineveh, according to the word of the Lord. Now Nineveh was an exceedingly great city, a three-day journey in extent. And Jonah began to enter the city on the first day's walk. Then he cried out and said, "Yet forty days, and Nineveh shall be overthrown"' (Jonah 3:3–4).

Whatever Jonah still felt within himself about the Ninevites, when the command came the second time he obeyed. But notice how the greatness, and extent and importance of the city are mentioned. This is emphasised again in the closing verse of the book when God says: 'And should I not pity Nineveh, that great city, in which are more than one hundred and twenty thousand persons who cannot discern between their right hand and their left—and much livestock?'

But why this emphasis upon the greatness and importance of Nineveh? It was indeed the greatest city of its day and the capital of the mighty Assyrian Empire. Bible scholars differ in their understanding of the three days required for a visit. Some think it refers to the circumference of the city, some sixty miles. Others understand the name Nineveh to comprise four small cities lying close together in the same region. Yet others are of the opinion that it took Jonah three days to walk from one end of the city to the other. If that is what actually happened then he would probably have stopped at various important places to preach the message God had given, so that the greater part of the population would have heard.

But the really important thing is not how big or great Nineveh was, but why God was so insistent that his voice should be heard in the city through the preaching of Jonah. It was because God saw the city as people; people lost in sin and wickedness, people without God and without hope in the world. The lesson here concerns urban evangelisation. Today, more and more people are leaving the countryside all over the world and are moving into the cities, and it is calculated that in the next fifteen years ninety per cent of the world's population will be living in urban areas.

Just think for the moment of mega-cities like Bombay, with its twenty eight million inhabitants, or Calcutta with its seventeen million, not to mention Shanghai, Beijing, New York, London, Paris and many other great cities of the world. Luke records the reaction of Jesus when he looked down on the city of Jerusalem. 'Now as he drew near, he saw the city and wept over it, saying, "If you had known, even you, especially in this your day, the things that make for your peace! But now they are hidden from your eyes"' (Luke 19:41–42). But why did Jesus weep? Because he saw the city not as a collection of fine buildings, or the centre of cultural and political life, but as people needing the peace of God's salvation and rejecting it. Lon Woodrum, a modern poet, expresses it well in the following:

> 'Cities are more than steel and stone, of humming
> wheels and towers alone, or busy shops and boulevards,
> or parks or home or well-kept yards.
>
> Cities are more than towering stores with neon-signs
> and countless doors.
>
> Cities have eyes awash with tears, and hearts that flee
> the mocking years.
>
> Cities are full of children crying and everywhere
> are people dying.
>
> Cities are more than stone-steel towers proudly
> proclaiming this technology of ours.
>
> Cities are people for whom Jesus cried. Cities are souls
> for whom he died'.

That is how God saw the great city of Nineveh, and how he sees the great cities of our world today, not as monuments to man's cleverness and technology, but as people needing to hear the good news of salvation.

That is how he wanted Jonah to see Nineveh, and he wants us to see our cities and towns, our villages and the urban areas in which our churches stand, in the same way.

The message preached

'And Jonah began to enter the city on the first day's walk. Then he cried out and said, "Yet forty days and Nineveh shall be overthrown"' (Jonah 3:4). We are not told a great deal about Jonah's sermon, simply the one sentence 'Forty days and Nineveh shall be overthrown'. We can be certain that his message was much longer than that. But it is significant that it is this particular sentence dealing with judgement that is given prominence. Why wasn't his message more evangelistic in content since he was there to convert people?

The reason is because the message of God's judgement is itself evangelistic. It is an evidence of God's mercy and grace, a warning to men and women of what awaits them if they do not repent. Peter says: 'He is longsuffering toward us, not willing that any should perish, but that all should come to repentance' (2 Peter 3:9). Why does the government put a health-warning on a packet of cigarettes? Is it because it wants to frighten people and spoil what they find pleasurable? No. It is the government's way of acting in the best interests of people by warning them of the risks involved. So it is with God's message of judgement; he desires to warn mankind of the consequences of sin, and does not want anyone to perish.

We must be careful, therefore, not to get carried away by the popular notion of being 'consumer friendly' in our preaching by not saying anything that would make the non-Christian in the congregation feel uncomfortable, and put them off Christianity. That would mean not saying anything about judgement, sin, or hell, or anything else that might lead them to think that God in Christ is not a wholly loving and gracious heavenly Father. But that is a very unbalanced view of God, and nowhere near the Bible's approach to evangelism. Following Peter's message on the day of Pentecost we read this: 'And with many other words he testified and exhorted them, saying, "Be saved from this perverse generation." Then those who gladly received his word were baptised, and that day about three thousand souls were added to them' (Acts 2:40–41). People were converted because they heeded the warning of God's judgement. Similarly, as we shall see, the people of Nineveh heeded Jonah's message of God's judgement. It follows that if we have a heart for the eternal welfare of people's souls, we will not hesitate to warn them of the dire consequences of rejecting God's salvation in the Lord Jesus Christ.

Nineveh's response

Read Jonah chapter 3:5–10

I n the preceding chapter we were concerned to make the point that the message of God's judgement is a necessary ingredient in evangelistic preaching. That ingredient was certainly effective in Jonah's preaching, and it set off a spiritual and moral earthquake in the city of Nineveh. 'So the people of Nineveh believed God, proclaimed a fast, and put on sackcloth, from the greatest to the least of them' (Jonah 3:5).

They believed God

We have no way of knowing if Jonah himself was surprised at the positive reception his preaching received from the people, but from my own experience in preaching I confess that it does amaze me that they received his message with such believing faith. After all, the people we are talking about were just about the most wicked and evil imaginable. According to the description of the prophet Nahum, the city was full of violence, lies, robbery, prostitution, witchcraft and idolatry. And yet, suddenly, under the preaching of God's word, we see this mass movement taking place, leading to national repentance and believing faith.

Now there are several things we can learn from this. In the first place it is only the sovereign grace of God that can bring about such a response. The people did not believe Jonah they believed God. That is, they accepted as true the message Jonah preached because it came to them from God. And Jonah himself was aware of that. For all his faults and disobedience he was God's prophet, and he believed intensely in the truth and power of the message he was called upon to deliver. He says as much later when he complains to God that he knew in advance that, if the Ninevites repented under his message, God would forgive them. 'Ah, Lord, was not this what I said when I was still in my own country? ... for I know that you are a gracious and merciful God, slow to anger and abundant in lovingkindness, one who relents from doing harm' (Jonah 4:2). In a strange way he was so certain of the effectiveness of his message to Gentiles that he did not want to preach it.

That poses the question to all preachers: Do we really believe in the message we preach, and are those we preach to aware of it? Do we believe that our message will be effective because it is God's word, and not simply our own ramblings? After all, God has given us a solid promise and assurance on that score. 'For as the rain comes down, and the snow from heaven, and do not return there, but water the earth, and make it bring forth and bud, that it may give seed to the sower and bread to the eater, so shall my word be that goes forth from my mouth; it shall not return to me void, but it shall accomplish what I please, and it shall prosper in the thing for which I sent it' (Isaiah 55:10–11).

God will always honour his word when it is faithfully declared. We *must* believe that whenever we enter the pulpit. His word will not return to him empty. We may not always see the effectiveness of that word in the salvation of souls, but that is not what is promised. God says that it will accomplish what he desires, not what we desire, and that it will achieve the purpose for which he sends it. That can be the purpose for people in the congregation being touched at different points in their lives. Some will be convicted of sin, others will be made to think seriously about the gospel for the first time, backsliders may be reclaimed, and believers will be strengthened and built up in their faith. The point is that faithful preaching of the word of God will never be a non-event, but will always accomplish something positive. We must believe that with all our heart, if we are to have confidence in our ministry.

Can anyone believe?

What happened at Nineveh should also teach us that we ought not to give up on the possibility that anyone can come to saving faith, even those whose lives are so profligate and wicked that we cannot imagine them ever coming to believe in the Lord Jesus Christ. Under Jonah's preaching people from all walks of life, young and old, from the ordinary citizen to the king and his nobles, believed the message. And that should be a great encouragement to us. If God, through the power of his word, could convict people like the Ninevites of their sin and of their need of repentance, then no one is beyond his reach.

And that is true not only of wicked and depraved people, but also of those who lead morally decent lives but who are totally indifferent to the claims of the gospel. We all know of those, perhaps in our own family, or friends, or colleagues at work, for whom we have been praying a long time regarding salvation, but with no result. The feeling can then be that the breakthrough will never come and we lose heart and are tempted to give up our praying and witnessing. But we must not do that. Remember that the response of the Ninevites was brought about entirely by the sovereign grace of God and we must rest on that. The Lord Jesus urges us to persevere in prayer. 'Then he (Jesus) spoke a parable to them, that men always ought to pray and not lose heart' (Luke 18:1).

They repented

'Then word came to the king of Nineveh; and he arose from his throne, and laid aside his robe, covered himself with sackcloth and sat in ashes. And he caused it to be proclaimed and published throughout Nineveh by the decree of the kings and his nobles, saying, "Let neither man nor beast, herd nor flock, taste anything; do not let them eat, or drink water. But let man and beast be covered with sackcloth, and cry mightily to God; yes, let every one turn from his evil way and from the violence that is in his hands. Who can tell if God will turn and relent, and turn away from his fierce anger, so that we may not perish?"' (Jonah 3:7–9).

The question is sometimes asked: Was the repentance of the Ninevites genuine in the sense that it led to salvation, or was it merely a moral reformation? Some commentators doubt its reality. 'Shall we say that the repentance of Nineveh was thoroughly spiritual and saving in the light of eternity? Alas, there is no evidence to show that thorough conversion to God was effected, at least in the city generally. True spiritual living religion does not seem even to have taken hold on Nineveh. Idolatry continued to be practised; and the ultimate fate of the city may be read in the prophecies of Nahum'. (Martin, *The Prophet Jonah,* Banner of Truth, 1958, p.272). Another writer states: 'it would appear that the revival was not long lasting. It was superficial, shallow, and short-lived; there was no deep moral reform, no change of heart, mind or disposition produced by God's Spirit and accompanied by sorrow arising from the sense of sin' (William L Banks, *Jonah the Reluctant Prophet,* Moody Press, 1966, pp. 96–97).

I find it difficult to go along with that point of view, if only because it implies that the destruction of Nineveh a hundred and fifty years later proves in some way that the people's repentance was not genuine. That surely is most unjust. But over and above that we have our Lord's commentary on the matter. 'The men of Nineveh will rise up in the judgement with this generation and condemn it, because they repented at the preaching of Jonah; and indeed a greater than Jonah is here' (Matthew 12:41). Why should Jesus have referred to Nineveh's repentance if it was not real? I agree wholeheartedly with Hendriksen when he says: 'If the repentance referred to in Matthew 12:41 is not genuine it is hard to explain the statement, 'the men of Nineveh will stand up at the judgement with this generation and condemn it'. Since it is the teaching of scripture (Daniel 7:22; Matthew 19:28; 1 Corinthians 6:2; Revelation 15:3) that God's children are going to participate in the final judgement, this statement of Jesus about the role of certain Ninevites in the Great Assize is understandable if their repentance was genuine' (Hendriksen, *Gospel of Matthew*, Banner of Truth, 1973, p. 536).

It follows that if their repentance was genuine, then their conversion was genuine as well. Perhaps not all repented to salvation, but some most certainly did.

What is Repentance?

The Bible teaches that repentance can be true or false. The apostle Paul puts it like this. 'For godly sorrow produces repentance leading to salvation, not to be regretted; but the sorrow of the world produces death' (2 Corinthians 7:10). False repentance is sorrow over the consequences of sin, being found out if you like, but not remorse over sin itself. And if the repentance is not genuine it cannot bring forgiveness of sins and therefore leads ultimately to death, eternal death. True repentance, on the other hand, involves a deep sense of contrition at having grieved God's Spirit, and leads to a change of mind for the better, bringing about a change of life and behaviour. If we look closely at the repentance of the Ninevites we can see that there were certain things about it that can only lead to the conclusion that it was real.

First, it was a popular spontaneous movement that began with the people and worked its way upward through every rank of society until it reached the king and his nobles. It was not something imposed on the people by a royal command. That only came later, when news of what was happening in the city reached the palace. Jonah, unlike Moses before Pharaoh, had no audience with the king, but began preaching to the ordinary people in the streets of the city on the very first day. 'And Jonah began to enter the city on the first day's walk. Then he cried out and said, "Yet forty days, and Nineveh shall be overthrown!" So the people of Nineveh believed God' (Jonah 3:4–5).

Second, there was a general fast among both men and animals. 'By the decree of the king and his nobles, saying, "Let neither man nor beast, herd nor flock, taste anything; do not let them eat, or drink water"' (Jonah 3:7). Why were the animals made to fast? To show total repentance. Domestic animals had a close relationship with men and were affected by what happened to them. Denying the animals food and water would cause them to bellow and cry out and, along with the people's fast, would demonstrate to God the intensity and seriousness of their repentance. Fasting therefore was a form of denial by turning aside for a while from the comforts and material concerns of life. Fasting is out of fashion these days among Christians, but the principle underlying it, to get away from all other distractions, including the preparation of food, in order to set the mind entirely upon God is still valuable and necessary. In a busy frenetic age like ours, we all have the need at times to revitalise the spiritual dryness that creeps into our Christian lives by shutting out all other demands, and spending time alone with God.

Third, they wore sackcloth. 'But let man and beast be covered with sackcloth'. They put away their fine fashionable clothes, the king even took off his royal robes, and they dressed in a coarse material, which was very unpleasant to wear. It was generally worn as a sign of mourning and distress, and on this occasion was meant to show God how penitent they were. We do not wear sackcloth today, but we may gain spiritually by adopting a simpler life-style. Clothes, fashion and the trinkets of modern consumerism are given far too high a priority in the lives of many Christians. John the Baptist was no fashion model when it came to clothes, and no gourmet when it came to food. 'Now John himself was clothed in camel's hair, with a leather belt around his waist; and his food was locusts and wild honey'. (Matthew 3:4). In the wilderness he had learned to cut life down to the basic essentials, so as to spend more time with God. And from that we can all learn to re-assess our priorities from time to time so as to be sure we are giving as much attention to the spiritual dimension of our lives as to the material.

Fourth, there was the use of dust and ashes. The king himself led the way in this. 'Then word came to the king of Nineveh; and he arose from his throne and laid aside his robe, covered himself with sackcloth and sat in ashes' (Jonah 3:6). Sitting in the dust and ashes, or sprinkling dust on one's head, signified humiliation and insignificance. When Nehemiah called for a day of national repentance in Judah we read: 'Now on the twenty-fourth day of this month the children of Israel were assembled with fasting, in wearing sackcloth, and with dust on their heads' (Nehemiah 9:1). Dust is also a reminder of our mortality: 'for dust you are, and to dust you shall return' (Genesis 3:19). It is no bad thing as Christians to keep in the forefront of our thinking the thought of our mortality, and of the brevity of life in this world compared with eternity. It will help us to keep a balanced view of life, and make us aware of how insignificant man is apart from God. James says, 'For what is your life? It is even a vapour and appears for a little time and then vanishes away' (James 4:14). Such a reminder will keep us humble, and we shall regard the need for repentance, and keeping short accounts with God, more seriously.

Fifth, they changed their behaviour. 'Yes, let every one turn from his evil way and from the violence that is in his hands. Who can tell if God will turn and relent, and turn away from his fierce anger, so that we may not perish?' (Jonah 3:8–9). We said earlier that true repentance leads to a change of mind for the better, leading to a change of behaviour. Well, here we have it with the Ninevites. But some are not even convinced with that, and complain that the people's repentance contained within it the element of fear of God's wrath, giving them unhealthy feelings of guilt. But why should people not feel guilty if they are wicked and sinful? Isn't that why we have a conscience? And isn't God's wrath a reality so that we are meant to fear his judgement upon us? But more importantly, the Ninevites were not only fearful where God was concerned, they were hopeful. 'Who can tell if God will turn and relent and turn away from his fierce anger, so that we may not perish'. The very fact that they were warned by Jonah's preaching of the reality of God's judgement, was itself an indication to them of God's mercy and his willingness to forgive.

And that is precisely what happened. 'Then God saw their works, that they turned from their evil way; and God relented from the disaster that he had said he would bring upon them, and he did not do it.' (Jonah 3:10). When God can see that our repentance is genuine and that we show it by our change of behaviour, he is very gracious and always ready to forgive us. That is the promise given in his word. 'If we confess our sins, he is faithful and just to forgive us our sins and to cleanse us from all unrighteousness' (1 John 1:9).

Did God change his mind?

Some Christians are troubled by what appears to be a contradiction between the positive message God gave to Jonah: 'forty days, and Nineveh shall be overthrown', and his willingness, when the people repented, not to bring upon them the destruction he had threatened. Does this mean that God changed his mind and his plans? We said earlier that God in himself is unchanging, and there are numerous scriptures to support that. 'For I am the Lord, I do not change' (Malachi 3:6). 'And also the strength of Israel will not lie nor relent. For he is not a man, that he should relent' (1 Samuel 15:29). Or this: 'Every good gift and every perfect gift is from above, and comes down from the Father of lights, with whom there is no variation or shadow of turning' (James 1:17).

So how do we meet this seeming contradiction? Well, we must keep in mind that the scriptures teach that God in his sovereignty knows all things and sees all things from the beginning, so that no event or circumstance can ever take him by surprise and cause him to revise his plans or change his mind. Earlier, when we dealt with God coming to Jonah the second time, we said that his purpose for Nineveh was the same as it had been the first time. He had not changed his mind, but gave Jonah the same instruction—that the people were to hear his word. God knew in advance what their response to that word would be; that they would repent, and therefore he did not change his mind when he dealt with them in a different way. This was a different Nineveh from the one on which he had pronounced his judgement. Then it was corrupt, wicked and impenitent. But now, after repentance, it was a humbled, penitent Nineveh which had turned away from its violence and wicked ways. All this was provided for in God's eternal plan, therefore he spared Nineveh.

But was it revival?

We have shown to our own satisfaction that the repentance of the Ninevites was genuine, leading to a real salvation experience, and was not simply a moral renewal. But having said that, we would not go along with those who believe that, because it was a spontaneous popular movement beginning with the people and containing the elements of prayer and preaching of the word, we can therefore describe it as a revival.

We are dealing here with a pagan people, not the people of God. Revival is a work of the Holy Spirit among God's own people. You cannot revive what is dead, only that which still has a flicker of life in it. Secular society is dead in its trespasses and sins, and needs to be quickened into spiritual life through the power of God's word. Revival, on the other hand, is the outpouring of the Holy Spirit upon the people of God, the church, for the revitalising of its spiritual life and worship. In times of revival the flicker of spiritual life is fanned to a flame so that God's people may become a more fitting instrument for him to use. Or, to put it another way, revival affects the church so that the church, in turn, may affect the world. We have a wonderful example of this in the Welsh revival.

During the 1904 revival in Wales, Evan Roberts, the young revivalist, introduced a prayer that was to become the theme of the revival: 'bend the church, and save the world'. The word 'bend' conveys the meaning of submission by God's people to his will. Evan Roberts was concerned to see the church revived under the power of the Holy Spirit so that it would become a mighty instrument in converting the unsaved. And that, in fact, is what happened. The number of those added to the churches throughout Wales was in the region of a hundred thousand. What happened in Nineveh was something totally different from revival. It was a wonderful example of urban evangelisation, which was greatly blessed of God in the conversion of many souls.

Jonah, an angry man

Read Jonah chapter 4:1–4

With the opening verses of this last chapter we come to the most extraordinary and bewildering part of the book of Jonah. We saw earlier that God had blessed his preaching to the Ninevites in a most remarkable way, by leading them to repentance and salvation. Moreover, in the light of his prayer inside the great fish—in which he was so thankful to God for his miraculous deliverance—we might have thought that his attitude towards the Gentile Ninevites would have changed, and that he would have been delighted at their repentance and God's forgiveness of them. Not a bit of it! Instead, he was terribly angry and upset.

'But it displeased Jonah exceedingly, and he became angry. So he prayed to the Lord, and said, "Ah, Lord, was not this what I said when I was still in my country? Therefore I fled previously to Tarshish; for I know that you are a gracious and merciful God, slow to anger and abundant in lovingkindness, one who relents from doing harm. Therefore now, O Lord, please take my life from me, for it is better for me to die than to live!" Then the Lord said, "Is it right for you to be angry?"' (Jonah 4: 1–4). Now is that not amazing? Here was a missionary or evangelist whose mission was a great success, and all he can do is moan and complain to God about it. It reminds me of a child's picture book belonging to my little grandson when he was about five years old, which had the intriguing title: 'Jonah the Moaner'. I can see why it was called that. But the question is how do we explain this moaning, complaining attitude of God's prophet?

Dying to self

We might put it all down to the fact that Jonah was a strange and complex personality, full of contradictory elements in his make-up, and simply leave it at that. But that is not good enough for at least three reasons. First, because he was God's servant and a preacher of the Word of God, the whole purpose of which is the saving of men and women like the Ninevites. Second, because he himself had experienced personally the grace and mercy of God in a most remarkable manner, and should not have denied it to others. Third, because these verses are not only an indictment of Jonah, but of ourselves. Like Jonah, we too are God's servants, we love the Lord Jesus Christ as our Saviour, and yet we exhibit all too often the same contradictory elements in our spiritual characters as he did in his. Here was the old Jonah, the old prejudiced, bigoted Jonah, which we had hoped had died in the great fish experience, rising to the surface again in this outburst of petulant anger and quarrelsomeness. And, we have to admit it, that same old, touchy, angry, sinful self is still very much alive in us. Jonah had not fully died to self, and neither have we if, we are perfectly honest. The truth is there are many deaths to die in the Christian life.

But does this mean that Jonah's prayer inside the great fish, his repentance, and his experience of God's grace and mercy towards him was all a sham? No, it does not mean that at all. It was all very real and sincere, just as our experience of God's grace in our lives is real. But that does not mean that Jonah, as God's servant, suddenly became perfectly holy, and all the sinful tendencies and instincts in his life were totally subdued. We know that cannot have been the case from our own spiritual experience. We have those times when our sense of the reality and nearness of God is so profound and moving that we feel we can reach out and touch him, as the chorus says.

> 'Open our eyes Lord,
> We want to see Jesus,
> To reach out and touch him
> And say that we love him.
> Open our ears Lord,
> And help us to listen:
> Open our eyes Lord,
> We want to see Jesus'.

But, real though that feeling is, there are other times when the old rampant, sinful self breaks through the surface of our lives in all its potential for evil, and any thought then of Christ is a million light years away. But why is that? Why do we have these contradictory elements deep within us which cause us, at times, to behave like two very different people? The Apostle Paul explains it like this: 'But you have not so learned Christ, if indeed you have heard him and have been taught by him, as the truth is in Jesus: that you put off, concerning your former conduct, the old man which grows corrupt according to the deceitful lusts, and be renewed in the spirit of your mind, created according to God, in true righteousness and holiness' (Ephesians 4:20–24).

But we all know what a difficult and painful business it is to keep that old self of ours under, and that our spiritual journey is rarely one of continual progress in holiness. Now it is true, as scripture says, 'that our old man was crucified' (Romans 6:6) with Christ when we first came to faith in him, but the sinful propensities, drives, and instincts of that old self are still very much alive in our bodies. We died to sin, when we were saved, but the principle of sin did not die in us, in our bodies. We still have many deaths to die in that sense. And this battle to destroy, or put to death, the tyranny of the old sinful self will continue as long as we live in this sinful world. But we are not alone in this. We have the indwelling Holy Spirit to help us grow more and more into the likeness of Christ. But a day is coming when the battle will end, and the tyranny of sin, even in our bodies, will be broken. Paul says we are to look forward to this, we are 'eagerly waiting for the adoption, the redemption of our body' (Romans 8:23).

Anger and the Christian

Jonah was angry, terribly angry because the Ninevites were not going to be destroyed after all. In fact, he was so angry that he even wanted to die and be rid of the whole rotten business. 'Therefore now, O Lord, please take my life from me, for it is better for me to die than to live!' (Jonah 4:3). Moreover, although he acknowledges that God is 'slow to anger', he himself had nevertheless been very quick to get angry. And we are like him in that too. Because it is a human emotion we all get angry at times. But is it ever right for the Christian to express that anger outwardly?

The scriptures have something to say about this. Writing to the Ephesians Paul says: '"Be angry, and do not sin": do not let the sun go down on your wrath' (Ephesians 4:26). Notice he does not condemn anger itself, but only when it is sinful. So there is a place for anger in the Christian life when it is of the right kind. Indeed, there were times when Jesus himself was terribly angry, as on the occasion when he healed a man's withered hand on the Sabbath day and the Pharisees present deeply resented it. We read: 'He had looked around at them with anger ...' (Mark 3:5). And he was majestically angry when he whipped the moneychangers and traders out of the temple (John 2:12–16). On both occasions Jesus was expressing a righteous anger or indignation; in the first instance, against the Pharisees indifference to needless suffering, and in the second instance against the desecration of God's house. This was a right kind of anger, and Christians are perfectly justified, in that sense, in showing anger against all sin and wickedness and injustice in the world.

Anger of the wrong kind—and which Paul is warning us against—is uncontrolled, selfish, full of lasting bitterness and the desire for revenge, and therefore sinful. Jonah's anger was of that kind. He was giving vent to his own spirit of rebellion and bitterness, and it was totally unjustified. That was why God said to him: 'Is it right for you to be angry?' (Jonah 4:4). He had no right whatsoever. We only have the right to be angry when our anger is not an expression of our own petulance and discontent, but is directed against everything that is evil in our world.

Angry with God

But with whom was Jonah angry in the first instance? With himself? No. With the Ninevites? Not initially. He was angry with God, and that is what made his anger sinful. But not only sinful, it was totally and utterly ridiculous. It is as though he said to God: 'I told you so, I knew this would happen, this saving of the Ninevites. If only you had listened to me in the first place'. 'Therefore I fled previously to Tarshish; for I know that you are a gracious and merciful God, slow to anger and abundant in lovingkindness, one who relents from doing harm' (Jonah 4:2). It sounds so silly and childish when it is put like that. Because getting angry with God is a sheer waste of time and effort, and gets you nowhere. And yet, like Jonah, we all get angry with God from time to time.

I recall when I was a young Christian I used to get very angry with God, because I felt he was not acting quickly enough, or that he had got things all wrong. But as I got older and became more spiritually mature I realised how futile it was, because we cannot influence God in any way by being angry with him. We have to rid ourselves of the idea that we can advise God, or browbeat him into changing his mind about something we do not agree with. We can plead with God, make requests of God, and seek to know his will and purpose, and in all these ways we can get somewhere. But the one thing we cannot do, and hope to achieve anything by it, is to get angry with God.

If we do, we can expect to get the same answer as Jonah: 'Is it right for you to be angry?' Because getting angry with God implies that we *do* have certain rights, rights which we think we have to defend and which God is obliged to take account of. But that is nonsense. In the climate of today's thinking the whole question of 'human rights' looms large, because there are rights which have to be defended in society; the rights of minorities, the poor and dispossessed, and so on. But where God is concerned we have no rights, none whatsoever. He owes us nothing, and he is not obligated to us in any way. He was under no obligation to extend to Jonah the privilege of being his spokesman and prophet, or to save him from the great fish, or to give him a renewed opportunity for service. It was all of his free grace. And so it is with us. We have no right to be angry. God could well say to us: 'don't you realise that all you have and are is because of my mercy and grace? Your creation, preservation and all the blessings of this life come from me. You owe me everything, but I owe you nothing'.

Worldly anger

It is on this question of anger that the non-Christian makes one of his profoundest mistakes where God is concerned. He asserts, either intellectually or by his life-style, that he has no interest in God, and yet he can get terribly angry when things go wrong in the world and he drags in God as a scapegoat for all these evils. He sees the suffering in the world, the injustices, the natural disasters with their great loss of life, and he says: 'Why does God allow it if he is a God of love and compassion?' But God's answer is exactly the same: 'Have you any right to be angry?' Indeed, God might well say to him: 'What arrogance, sinful man, that you with your selfishness, your crass-materialism, your power-mania, your warring and fighting, your obsession with sex and violence, your pride and deceit should be angry with me, and talk of your rights when you have not a leg to stand on. The world is in the spiritual and moral pile-up that it is precisely because of your sin and disobedience. You, with your pride in your technology and scientific advancement, have not even found a way of living together peacefully as yet, but you have the audacity to get angry with me, the living God, and talk about your rights!'

Eugene O'Neill the playwright, not a Christian, put it more bluntly in an interview. 'If the human race is so stupid that in two thousand years it has not had brains enough to appreciate that the secret of happiness is contained in one simple sentence which you would think any schoolboy could understand and apply, then it is time we dumped it down the nearest drain and let the ants have a chance. That simple sentence is: "For what will it profit a man if he gain the whole world and lose his own soul?"'

What it comes down to in the end is this. If anyone wants to know why our world is in the mess it is, and why God acts in the way he does, then there has to be a radical change of attitude. It is no use getting angry with God. What is required is a willingness to be more humble and contrite, and to realise that whereas we need God, he certainly does not need us. We need his mercy, his forgiveness and his grace revealed to us in Christ and his gospel. And when we come there, and are willing to accept that, then we begin to get some of the answers we are looking for.

Why was Jonah angry?

There may be more than one reason underlying his anger. Undoubtedly the most important of these was God's refusal to do what Jonah wanted him to do. Jonah did not want the Ninevites forgiven and converted because he hated Gentiles, and the Ninevites in particular were the enemy of his own people. He wanted to see them destroyed, and by his rebellion in refusing to go to Ninevah at the outset he had hoped to influence or manipulate God into agreeing with that. But the strategy failed. God would not be manipulated and Ninevah was spared destruction. Do we get angry with God for the same reason? Because he does not do what we want him to do? Like Jonah we have our little strategies to manipulate God to adjust to our way of thinking, and some of them are quite childish. We refuse to attend the worship of his house, or we give up praying or reading the Bible.

This kind of behaviour is no different from the way tribal people manipulated their idol gods. If the god did not give them the rain they asked for, or do some other thing they wanted badly, they became very angry and destroyed the idol and made a new one. And there is a sense in which people today do the same thing with the modern gods of man's making: sport, moneymaking, sex, politics etc. They manipulate these things to provide the satisfaction they require, and when this fails, or the satisfaction comes to an end, they get very disillusioned and discontented and discard these 'gods' for something else. We must understand as Christians, for our own good and peace of mind, that God cannot be manipulated, controlled, or made to adjust to our thinking. He can only be obeyed.

Second, I suspect that somewhere along the line Jonah was angry with God because maybe his pride was wounded. He was a prophet and preacher and had proclaimed that Ninevah would be destroyed in forty days. And now that was not going to happen. Instead they were to be forgiven. And these were the inveterate enemy of his own people! I wonder if he felt a bit foolish and embarrassed at the turn events had taken? And what of his reputation as a prophet?

Pride is the darling sin and usually lies at the bottom of most of our wrongdoing. We can get very angry when our pride is wounded, our dignity offended, or our reputation suffers in the eyes of others. But again the same question is addressed to us: 'Is it right for you to be angry?' That is, have we the right to get so up-tight about our self-esteem when we remember the humility of Christ? He left the royalty of heaven and the Father's side and came into the world where he became the butt of sinners. When the disciples were standing on their dignity in the upper room refusing to serve one another, he knelt and washed their feet. Or this: 'Who, being in the form of God, did not consider it robbery to be equal with God, but made himself of no reputation, taking the form of a bondservant, and coming in the likeness of men. And being found in appearance as a man, he humbled himself and became obedient to the point of death, even the death of the cross!' (Philippians 2:6–8). How cheap and tawdry our human pride and self-esteem appears in light of that!

Third, Jonah was angry because, in spite of his being a prophet and preacher of the Lord, he did not have deep down that burden for the souls of his fellowmen, which every preacher ought to have. He had no interest whatever in being 'a light to lighten the Gentiles'. His Jewish prejudice, his bigotry and narrow-mindedness led him to believe, sincerely I have no doubt, that he alone was the defender and guardian of Israel's spiritual life. His inner blindness in that respect was such that he actually said he preferred to die rather than live and see the Ninevites saved. He said in effect to God: 'life will not be worth living if you are now going to start saving Gentiles as well. I want out!'

The terribly sad thing was that he knew better than most the true heart of God. 'I know that you are a gracious and merciful God, slow to anger and abundant in lovingkindness, one who relents from doing harm' (Jonah 4:2). He knew that! Moreover he himself had been at the receiving end of that love and compassion in a wonderful way. And yet, in spite of all that, he could not find it in his deepest heart to show the slightest tenderness of feeling towards the Ninevites. Let us make no mistake about it, prejudice and bigotry is a pernicious disease especially when found in believers. It can distort our thinking, blind us to what is good and lovely, make us comfortable in our self-complacency, and even harden us towards the spiritual needs of others so that we have no burden for their souls. May the good Lord save us from that.

God's questions

Read Jonah chapter 4:5–11

O ur previous chapter ended at verse 4 with God asking Jonah a question. 'Is it right for you to be angry?' In this section we immediately notice that Jonah gave no answer. Perhaps he did not have an answer, or he was not in the mood to answer, or else his refusal to answer was his way of showing God how angry he really was. Be that as it may, later—when God puts the same question to him again—he answers in a very positive manner. 'Then God said to Jonah, "Is it right for you to be angry about the plant?" And he said "It is right for me to be angry, even to death"' (Jonah 4:9). We can assume from this very strong response that, whatever the reason for his silence the first time, on the inside he felt certain that this anger was perfectly justified, and he proceeded to show it by what he did next.

'So Jonah went out of the city and sat on the east side of the city. There he made himself a shelter, and sat under it in the shade, till he might see what would become of the city' (Jonah 4:5). What a strange thing for him to have done, especially in view of the fact that the people of Nineveh had repented, and the city was no longer going to be destroyed. We shall say something about that in a moment, but first we must look at a matter which some Christians find very puzzling.

Informing God?

Why does God ask questions? For the book of Jonah, unlike any other book in the Old Testament, even ends with God asking a question but giving no answer. 'And should I not pity Nineveh, that great city, in which are more than one hundred and twenty thousand persons who cannot discern between their right hand and their left—and much livestock?' (Jonah 4:11). Some Christians find it all very confusing, since one of God's greatest attributes is his omniscience—he is all knowing. When *we* ask questions it is because we do not know everything, and we need to be informed by someone who may come up with the answers. But God does

not need to be informed by anyone. As Paul rightly says: 'Oh, the depth of the riches both of the wisdom and knowledge of God! How unsearchable are his judgements, and his ways past finding out! "For who has known the mind of the Lord? Or who has become his counsellor?" Or who has first given to him and it shall be repaid to him?" For of him and through him and to him are all things, to whom be glory forever. Amen' (Romans 11:34–36).

And it is not only in the book of Jonah that God asks questions, he does so all through the Old Testament. We read in Genesis: 'And they heard the sound of the Lord God walking in the garden in the cool of the day, and Adam and his wife hid themselves from the presence of the Lord God among the trees of the garden. Then the Lord God called to Adam and said to him, "Where are you?" So he said, "I heard your voice in the garden, and I was afraid because I was naked; and I hid myself"' (Genesis 3: 8–10). Why did God need to ask, 'Where are you?' Was it because Adam and Eve had hidden themselves so successfully that God could not find them? Of course not. The purpose of the question was to reinforce in their minds the enormity of their sin and disobedience, and to bring them out into the open and confess it.

And so it is with all God's questions. They are meant to teach us something, or to expose to us our inner selves when we are guilty of sin or disobedience. When God asked Cain: 'Where is Abel your brother?' (Genesis 4:9), it was not because God was not aware that Abel had been killed, but to bring home to Cain the callousness of his heart in murdering his brother. Or take the case of Job. He had challenged God with many questions criticising his justice and his government of the world. But at the end of the book (Job chapters 38–40), God turns the tables on Job and fires a whole string of questions at him—some sixty in all—dealing with the origin of the universe, the control of the seas and tides, and the movement of the constellations and planets. He begins with the question: 'Where were you when I laid the foundation of the earth?' (Job 38:4). God wants to humble Job and teach him, and the rest of us, that man with his limited knowledge is in no position to question or criticise God's government of the universe.

So whenever we read the Bible and come across God asking a question, we ought to ask ourselves, 'Is God addressing that question to me, and if so what am I meant to learn from it?'

The folly of resentment

Now to come back to Jonah's weird behaviour in going outside the city, 'So Jonah went out of the city and sat down on the east side of the city. There he made himself a shelter and sat under it in the shade, till he might see what would become of the city' (Jonah 4:5). What on earth was he doing now? Well, his anger had now passed the boiling point, and instead it had settled down to a deep brooding resentment towards God and, I suppose, towards the people of Nineveh. He was hoping perhaps that God would think again and withdraw his forgiveness, and still destroy Nineveh and punish the people. In the meantime, in the black mood he was in, he was prepared to sit and wait under the burning sun, in isolation and distinctly uncomfortable, and with his resentment festering away inside his system like a poison. We may feel a bit fed up with him at this point and wonder to ourselves: 'what kind of a prophet is he? Why does he not accept that it is all over? God's decision on Nineveh stands, so he might as well pack up and go home to Garth Hepher.'

But that is the awful thing about a spirit of resentment when it gets a hold on us. We nurse it, brood upon it, hug it close to us. At the same time it makes us increasingly unhappy and miserable, because resentment towards anyone always hurts us more than the other person. And it can happen to any of us. We get angry and uptight about something or someone and, instead of dealing with it right away, we allow it to fester within us distorting our whole personality and making us impossible to live with, and unable to worship God aright. That is why the apostle says: 'Do not let the sun go down on your wrath' (Ephesians 4:26). If we do not kill the anger in the early stages, but end the day with it still dominating our thinking, it will turn into a deep-seated resentment that poisons the whole system.

Jesus also had something to say about this in the form of a parabolic saying. 'Agree with your adversary quickly, while you are on the way with him, lest your adversary deliver you to the judge, the judge hand you over to the officer, and you be thrown into prison. Assuredly, I say to you, you will by no means get out of there till you have paid the last penny' (Matthew 5:25–26). The point Jesus is making is that when we have fallen out with someone, or even with God himself, the time for putting matters right in the relationship is NOW, not next week or next month, or it may be too late. The brooding beast of resentment within us may destroy any desire we might have for reconciliation, and we may be suddenly called from this life to stand before the eternal judge in the heavenly court with that resentful spirit still in our heart. And that is a dreadful thought!

The Spectator

There is another slant on this strange behaviour of Jonah. He sat under his shelter as a spectator of Nineveh and its people. 'There he made himself a shelter and sat under it in the shade, till he might see what would become of the city' (Jonah 4:5). It almost beggars belief that as a prophet and preacher of God's word he should sit on the sidelines, as it were, in judgement and criticism of the Ninevites, instead of participating or being involved with them in their repentance and desire to experience God's saving grace in their lives. It reminds me of those occasions when we are on holiday, perhaps in France or Italy, and we spend some time at a pavement café drinking a cup of coffee and just watching the world go by. We are not *doing* anything, we are simply spectators. And that is perfectly legitimate as a holiday pastime. But at the spiritual level we dare not adopt that spectator view of life, and watch the world go by from the shelter and security of our own position in Christ, without getting involved in any way with its challenges and sufferings.

That is to totally misunderstand the role of the Christian in relation to the world, and it does violence to the teaching of the gospel on the whole question of separation from the world. The monastic-principle, that you shut yourself off from the demands and temptations of secular society and retire to a life of seclusion and contemplation, is nowhere to be found in the New Testament. On the contrary, the Lord Jesus tells us quite specifically that we are to be the 'salt of the earth', and 'the light of the world' (Matthew 5:13–14). Moreover in his High Priestly prayer in which he prays for believers Jesus says: 'I do not pray that you should take them out of the world, but that you should keep them from the evil one. … As you sent me into the world, I also have sent them into the world' (John 17:15–18).

It is perfectly clear that the Christian is meant to be in the world, but not of the world. We are to function as salt and light in the midst of all the rottenness and darkness of our modern society. And there is no denying that there is today a strong stench of putrefaction and moral decay in that society, and that a good stiff dose of the gospel's antiseptic would do it the power of good. Likewise our world is in a state of darkness, not intellectual darkness since we have made enormous strides in the understanding of our world and its environment through our science and technology. But spiritually and morally society is still very much in darkness, and the powers of evil are working overtime.

As believers in the Lord Jesus and his gospel we are meant to be a light in that darkness by the kind of life we live. We are to expose the emptiness and futility of the world's way by showing in our own lifestyle that there are other values and standards, other hopes and aspirations, that can enable us to fulfil the potential of our humanity as those made in the image of God. We can never be spectators therefore, and simply watch the world go by. On God's behalf we are to be participants in the life of the world, not in order to be like it, but to change it.

Jonah and the plant

As he sits under his shelter Jonah is in a bad way spiritually and physically. He is mentally exhausted, his emotions are in a turmoil, and to add to his discomfort the sun beats down on him mercilessly. But God is very gracious to his servant, and wants to teach him that things can be very different. In the first place he wants Jonah to understand that, in spite of his prejudice and disobedience, he still loves him and cares about him, and is concerned for his physical well-being and comfort. So we read: 'And the Lord God prepared a plant and made it come up over Jonah, that it might be shade for his head to deliver him from his misery. So Jonah was very grateful for the plant' (Jonah 4:6).

We are glad to see Jonah happy and grateful for once. Earlier we had described him as Jonah the moaner, because from the time God had called him to go to Nineveh he had done nothing but moan and complain about God's purposes. But now he was happy because God was doing something for him personally by providing the plant to give him shade from the sun. And that carries its own message about how thankful and happy we should be that God is a loving heavenly Father who, by his providential care, does so much for us personally. He is not only mindful of our souls in the provision of salvation in Christ, but he also cares about our physical well-being and our material welfare. At the dawn of creation when God created man we read: 'God blessed them and said to them, "Be fruitful and multiply; fill the earth and subdue it; have dominion over the fish of the sea, over the birds of the air, and over every living thing that moves on the earth"' (Genesis 1:28).

That is God's 'cultural mandate' to man, giving him the right to govern and control the earth with all its intricate processes and complex systems. He is the steward of the earth's resources to use them for his own benefit. The Bible therefore is in no way anti-material, or anti-culture, or anti-knowledge. Man is to use his science and technology under God to subdue and rule the earth, and to enjoy its material and physical blessings for his own pleasure and enjoyment. But as a result of man's sin and disobedience what we see happening today is that man does not give thanks to God for his providential care, and he abuses his environment, and wastes the natural gifts and resources God has given him.

But beyond showing Jonah that he cares about his material and physical well-being, God had other truths he wanted to teach him, and to do that he performed two other miracles.

The worm and the east wind

'But as morning dawned the next day God prepared a worm, and it so damaged the plant that it withered. And it happened, when the sun arose, that God prepared a vehement east wind; and the sun blazed on Jonah's head, so that he grew faint. Then he wished death for himself, and said, "It is better for me to die than to live". Then God said to Jonah, "Is it right for you to be angry about the plant?" And he said "It is right for me to be angry, even to death!"' (Jonah 4:7–9). Jonah now is not only angry, but is in a real state of emotional distress. He is profoundly miserable, and in danger of sinking into deep spiritual depression. But all that God did was very deliberate on his part. He deliberately 'prepared' the worm to destroy the plant and the east wind to make life so unbearable for Jonah that he considered it better to die than to live. But what was God seeking to accomplish in all this?

First, he wanted to humble Jonah, and to bring him to that point where he would be made to realise that he had been far too wrapped up in himself, in his own stubbornness and prejudice as if everything had depended on him, and not on God. In his mistaken nationalistic zeal he had taken on himself the role of defender of Israel's faith, as if God were somehow failing in that. It was as if he felt it was up to him to save God from his own folly and mistaken purpose in wanting to preserve Nineveh and save its people. But this was sheer arrogance on Jonah's part, and God was not going to tolerate it for one moment. So he performed one miracle in providing Jonah with the plant to keep him happy, and then he performed another miracle to take the plant away and to make him miserable. In that way he was teaching Jonah who was in charge, that he is the sovereign eternal God, and that Jonah is totally dependent on him and not he on Jonah.

We must be careful not to give way to the idea that somehow God is dependent on us, that we are indispensable to his cause, and that without our input that cause will fail. That is sheer conceit and nonsense, yet we can all behave occasionally as though that were true. We try to do God's thinking for him. Even Abraham tried that when he married Hagar who gave birth to Ishmael, and—when the promised son was born—the basis was laid for all the hatred and hostility in Middle East politics today between Arabs and Jews. We must learn that we are not indispensable for the working-out of God's purposes in the world. Like the provision of the plant, he can raise us up and use us at one moment, and—should it please him—he can stop using us the next. God is in charge, and we are totally dependent on him. As the saying goes: 'God buries his workmen but he carries on his work'. That is a humbling thought, and we need to keep it in the forefront of our thinking, because it will help us to see our place in the overall plan of God in a realistic way.

Distorted values

Second, God wanted to teach Jonah about his distorted sense of values and wrong order of priorities. 'But the Lord said, "You have had pity on the plant for which you have not laboured, nor made it grow, which came up in a night and perished in a night. And should I not pity Nineveh, that great city, in which are more than one hundred and twenty thousand persons who cannot discern between their right hand and their left—and much livestock?' (Jonah 4:10–11). The plant had made life more comfortable and pleasant for Jonah, and had contributed to his sense of personal well-being, but by removing it God had exposed his selfishness and distorted sense of values in putting his own material concerns before the spiritual needs of the Ninevites. For Jonah, the plant was more important than people.

Jesus warns us more than once about getting our view on life out of perspective in this way. 'Therefore I say to you, do not worry about your life what you will eat or what you will drink; nor about your body, what you will put on. Is not the life more than food and the body more than clothing?' (Matthew 6:25). Or this: 'For what will it profit a man if he gains the whole world, and loses his own soul?' (Mark 8:36). For we can all be guilty of giving greater prominence and value to the things we surround ourselves with, and which give us pleasure and make life pleasant, than to the needs of others and the demands of the gospel. Like Jonah we can so easily get our priorities mixed up, so that material things take over our lives and absorb our time and energies, while God's concern must surely be the salvation of the souls of men and women. Is not that the implication of his question to Jonah? 'And should I not pity Nineveh, that great city, in which are more than one hundred and twenty thousand persons who cannot discern between their right hand and their left—and much livestock?' (Jonah 4:11).

God's pity and ours

But to whom exactly is God's pity and compassion directed when he speaks of those 'who cannot discern between their right hand and their left?' For some commentators maintain that it refers to infants too young to know the difference physically between their right and left hands, and therefore between good and bad. But I cannot go along with that, if only because it is not only children who are unable to discern right from wrong. In the light of the context it seems certain that the expression refers to the spiritual and moral ignorance of the whole population of Nineveh. That, after all, was why God instructed Jonah to go to the city in the first place: 'for their wickedness has come up before me' (Jonah 1:2). God loves people, even people as wicked and evil as those of Nineveh. That is why he pities them in their spiritual and moral ignorance and desires to save them.

The fact was that Jonah had a great zeal for God's honour, and believed it was best served by the destruction of the Gentile Ninevites. But God had to teach him that it was a zeal without knowledge—the knowledge of his pity and compassion for all mankind, and not only for the Jews. Paul in his day made the same complaint about his fellow-Jews. 'For I bear them witness that they have a zeal for God, but not according to knowledge. For they being ignorant of God's righteousness, and seeking to establish their own righteousness, have not submitted to the righteousness of God (Romans 10:2, 3). That speaks to us. Sincerity and zeal in the Christian life is highly commendable, but it is insufficient on its own. It has to be based on an adequate understanding of the revealed truth in God's word; otherwise it can lead to spiritual arrogance, an unteachable spirit, and even fanaticism.

The other important point in God's question is the reference to livestock. God's pity and compassion extends, not only to the people of Nineveh, but to the cattle. What is the significance of that? Well, in Biblical times sheep and cattle represented a man's wealth and substance. Abraham we are told, 'was very rich in livestock, in silver and gold' (Genesis 13:2). The reference therefore might simply mean that God is concerned not only with the spiritual aspect of life, but with man's physical and material well-being. Speaking of God's providence the Psalmist says, 'You preserve man and beast' (Psalm 36:6).

But perhaps we should also see, in this reference to cattle, God's care and concern for man's total environment. We learn from Genesis that when God created the animal kingdom, he not only declared it to be good, but he blessed the animals as well (Genesis 1:21–22). And in Psalm 148 the whole created order, including the animals, are called upon to praise God and to show forth his glory. The book of Jonah therefore could be reminding us that ecology is important to God, and should in turn be important to us as his people. We are the stewards of God's creation. When man loses sight of the Creator, as he has done today, it is inevitable that he should think that he can do as he likes with creation, and that explains the terrible destruction he is bringing on the natural order.

But why does the book of Jonah end so abruptly, with a question and no answer? God asks: 'and should I not pity Nineveh, that great city, in which are more than one hundred and twenty thousand persons who cannot discern between their right hand and their left—and much livestock?' (Jonah 4:11). And the question is left hanging in the air, as it were. Is this because God wants each of us to answer that question for him or her self? Does God want us to say something like this in reply? 'Yes Lord, it is right and proper that you should show pity and compassion for the salvation of the people of Nineveh, and all those other lost souls in our world who know nothing of your salvation. And you want us to make that salvation known through the preaching of the gospel and by our personal witness to what you have done in our lives'. Is not that the kind of answer God wants?

After all, that is the whole burden of the book of Jonah, to create in our hearts a missionary and evangelistic concern for people's souls as great as his pity and compassion for Nineveh. The Ninevites are all around us in our modern world, people who are so spiritually blind that they 'cannot discern between their right hand and their left'. The big question is, who is concerned about their immortal souls? The government? Social Services? The entertainment industry? Big business? These all have their legitimate objectives and they are perfectly right to pursue them. But our objective as believers must be people's eternal welfare. God has addressed man's destiny in the gospel of his Son the Lord Jesus Christ, and he has given us the privilege and responsibility of making that gospel known.

> Go forth and tell! O church of God, awake!
> God's saving news to all the nations take:
> Proclaim Christ Jesus, Saviour, Lord, and King,
> That all the world his worthy praise may sing.
>
> Go forth and tell! Men still in darkness lie:
> In wealth or want, in sin they live and die:
> Give us, O Lord, concern of heart and mind,
> A love like yours which cares for all mankind.
> James E. Seddon

One final question as we bring this exposition to a close. Did Jonah take to heart the lessons God was teaching him, since we are not told of any response he may have made? All through the book he has had a lot to say by way of argument with God. But now he is silent. Was he shamed into silence? Had he come to believe at last that God was right all along? For God always has the last word. When wicked men crucified the Lord of glory they thought they had the last word. But the resurrection showed how wrong they were. Where Jonah was concerned I believe he did in fact take those lessons on board. As we said at the outset, he wrote this book. And that means that—with great deliberation and honesty—he put on record this account of how God, in mercy and grace, dealt with his prejudice and disobedience, so that we may learn from his mistakes. May God help us to do just that.